HUMILITY

C. PETER WAGNER

Regal

From Gospel Light
Ventura, California, U.S.A.

Published by Regal Books
From Gospel Light
Ventura, California, U.S.A.
Printed in the U.S.A.

Cover and Internal Design by Robert Williams
Edited by Steven Lawson

LIBRARY OF CONGRESS CATALOGING-IN-PUBLICATION DATA
Wagner, C. Peter.
    Humility / C. Peter Wagner.
        p. cm.
    ISBN 0-8307-2935-6 (hardcover)
    ISBN 0-8307-3057-5 (paperback)
    1. Humility—Christianity. I. Title.
    BV4647.H8 W34 2002
    241'.4—dc21   2001007606

1 2 3 4 5 6 7 8 9 10 11 12 13 14 15 / 09 08 07 06 05 04 03 02

Rights for publishing this book in other languages are contracted by Gospel Light Worldwide, the international nonprofit ministry of Gospel Light. Gospel Light Worldwide also provides publishing and technical assistance to international publishers dedicated to producing Sunday School and Vacation Bible School curricula and books in the languages of the world. For additional information, visit www.gospellightworldwide.org; write to Gospel Light Worldwide, P.O. Box 3875, Ventura, CA 93006; or send an e-mail to info@gospellightworldwide.org.

CONTENTS

WHOEVER EXALTS HIMSELF

WILL BE HUMBLED,

AND WHOEVER HUMBLES HIMSELF

WILL BE EXALTED.

Matthew 23:12, *NIV*

GETTING SERIOUS

For anyone who has been a committed Christian for some time, humility, the subject of this book, is familiar ground. Or is it?

Here is the reason I raise the question: It could well be that humility, of all the frequently mentioned and highly respected Christian virtues, might take a prize as the least *analyzed* of them all. The subject of humility seems to carry with it some kind of uncomfortable baggage of insecurity or inadequacy.

SERMONS ON HUMILITY?

Let's begin by thinking about this virtue in a new way. Take a few moments to recall some of the hundreds, perhaps thousands, of sermons that you have heard. How many of those teachings dealt with the subject of humility—*from beginning to end?* As I was preparing to write this book, I asked that question to many of my friends. None of them could remember preaching or hearing someone else preach a whole sermon on humility.

For many it seemed strange that it was actually hard to rec-ollect such a sermon, because none of them had any problem remembering countless other teachings in which humility had been prominently mentioned. This virtue, in the sense that we all need to be humble, is common currency among preachers. There is no debate that humility pleases God. We all agree that pride, the opposite of humility, can get us into a lot of trouble. Everyone is supposed to know this fundamental principle; therefore, there is a supposition that everyone also under-stands the ins and outs of it. But few ever take it beyond this broad and misplaced assumption.

ANDREW MURRAY

For the most part, pastors tend to have large personal libraries. Therefore, test what I have asserted and ask your pastor how many books on the explicit subject of humility he or she has in his or her library. Although there may be an exception here or there, the chances are that you will get either one of two responses. The first is "I don't really have any." They might add "However, I do have some books that stress humility, although the word is not in the title." These books do not count. The second response might be "I have one—I have Andrew Murray's book."

Murray's book, *Humility*, is the widely regarded classic on the subject. There are two very interesting things about his book. First, it virtually stands alone. Whether copies are in their libraries or not, most practicing pastors are at least aware of it. Those who are familiar with Murray's work will frequently say, "It's the best book on humility that I know of." This would be true because, for the most part, they are not aware of any other book on the subject. Their libraries may contain several books on healthy marriages, prayer and reaching the new generation;

they may include texts on the second coming of Christ, worship and spiritual gifts—but not on humility.

I would note, in passing, that through the ages humility has been a more explicit and high-profile element of Roman Catholic piety than of Protestant spirituality. The majority of the 60-some books with the word "humility" in the title on the Amazon.com list, other than Murray's book, are by Catholic authors. Murray's *Humility* appears on the list in six editions!

The second interesting factor about Murray's book is that it was written 100 years ago! By this I do not mean that his ideas are antiquated. If they were, it would not still be in print. It has the qualities of a classic—and the subject of humility will never get old. Nevertheless, it seems strange that nearly six generations later we have no expanded library on humility, at least among Protestants.

Why not? Why have more Protestant Christian authors not adopted humility as a topic for research, analysis and writing? I have some clues regarding a possible answer to this question that I will note a bit later. In fact, that is one of the purposes I have in embracing a task that many prefer keeping at arm's length: writing a book such as this.

THE FOUNDATIONAL TEXT

Many people will agree with my selection of the foundational biblical text for understanding humility—the words of Jesus in Matthew 23:12 (*NIV*):

> Whoever exalts himself *will be humbled*, and whoever humbles himself *will be exalted* (emphasis added).

In this short Scripture passage we find two parallel pairs of active and passive verbs. By *active verbs*, I mean actions that we must *choose* to initiate. If we do not decide to do this certain thing, it simply will not happen, regardless of what we may know theologically to be God's perfect will. That is so important that I will be coming back to this thought again and again. In other words, it basically depends upon us!

On the other hand, the *passive verb* does not depend on us at all. If we decide, rightly or wrongly, to do the active verb, the passive thing will inevitably happen to us whether we want it to or not. We might say that the active takes *human* initiative, while the passive takes *divine* initiative. Let's think about the active verbs first.

The Active Verb: Humble Yourself

The point I want to make here is that humility is a matter of a personal choice. Are you humble? If you are, it is because you have decided that you will be humble. If you are not, it is because you have not decided to be humble. I realize that what I have just said may sound simplistic. But the Bible refers to humbling yourself, and that is very simple language. It is an active verb.

Another way of saying this is that humility has to be *attained.* I hope that this book helps you take the trip to humility, so to speak, and actually arrive. Suppose that you desire to go to San Antonio, Texas. You look it up on a map, choose the appropriate mode of transportation, set aside some time, find the money, take the trip and arrive at your destination. You go about attaining humility in just about the same way.

I would imagine that some readers, at this point in the first chapter, are beginning to wonder if the direction I am heading is really biblical. I can sympathize with that concern because we have not been hearing many of our pastors or other Christian leaders say things such as this quite so plainly. In fact, many of them have been thinking just the opposite.

CLERGY HUMOR AND HUMILITY

If you are a pastor or if you have been around pastors very much, you will recognize this scenario: A group of pastors hangs out together. They drink coffee, eat some sweets and have a good time. Suddenly, a big smile forms on the face of one pastor and he says, "Hey, guys, I just finished my new book: *Humility and How I Attained It!*" Everybody has a good laugh! I suppose that I have personally heard this at least a half dozen times. It has become a standard clergy joke.

> Pastors feel secure about preaching on the broad virtue of humility, but they often feel insecure when it comes to the specific practical application of it in their own lives.

A joke? Why would this be regarded as humorous? It is considered a laughing matter because, among pastors, it is commonly assumed that none of them could ever truly be humble. Moreover, saying that they themselves *attained* humility would be seen as an expression of pride and therefore, ipso facto, nullify any humility that might have been achieved.

What this exhibits is a curious underlying nervousness among Christian leaders about the subject of humility. Pastors feel secure about preaching on the broad virtue of humility, but they often feel insecure when it comes to the specific practical application of it in their own lives. Why? In my opinion it is because they lack basic knowledge. I cannot remember a single lesson on humility in all the seminary classes that I took. As I have already mentioned, hardly anyone preaches whole sermons on the subject of humility. Our collective understanding of all the ramifications of humility, strange as it may seem, is considerably low.

CLOTHED WITH HUMILITY?

The Bible, however, is deceptively straightforward on the subject. For example, look at what Peter says: "Yes, all of you be submissive to one another, and be clothed with humility" (1 Pet. 5:5). This is an interesting metaphor. Being humble is, apparently, like getting dressed. Who puts *your* clothes on each morning? You do! You are not naked at this moment because *you* decided to put clothes on and *you* dressed yourself. In the same way, we all are supposed to be *clothed* with humility. It is the active verb again. We must decide to do it, and then do it!

As you read this you would have no problem in truthfully saying "I am dressed." Likewise, many Christian readers would comfortably say, in appropriate contexts, "I am a tither," "I am faithful to my spouse," "I pray every day," or "I go to church on Sundays." Each one of these statements, and many others like them, is actually expected of anyone who is trying to please God and live a good Christian life. But try this one: "I am humble." For some reason it does not sound exactly the same as the other statements. It seems to create a subtle dissonance. It feels quite uncomfortable to say this, even though everyone knows that we are supposed to be humble.

I think this is a major reason why we do not hear more sermons on the subject. When we are uncomfortable with a subject, it is very hard to preach on it. Furthermore, preachers know that people expect them to be role models. I heard one pastor say, "I'm struggling with my humility!" But I never heard the same man say "I'm struggling with tithing!" or "I'm struggling with being faithful to my wife!" One of the deadly sins of preachers is to say "Do as I say, but do not do as I do!"

The Passive Verb: God Humbles You

If the active verb, for the person being humbled, is "humble yourself," the passive verb is "God humbles you." (By this I mean that it is passive for the recipient, although technically it is still an active verb.)

Let's do a quick review: If we choose to be humble (active) we end up exalted (passive). This combination has an interesting implication that we might not always think about. If we are, in fact, exalted, we must be humble. Why? If we were not humble, God would not have exalted us. Is this what the Bible says?

Because of my age and years of Christian leadership, I have had the privilege of personally knowing a large number of highly respected Christian leaders. Every one of them is a humble person. I know that, at first glance, not all of them communicate that virtue in public. That is why many who relate to certain leaders only through their television shows, through keynote messages in conferences, through books they publish or through articles written about them in the media may come to the conclusion that they are proud people. I understand this because I have formed similar opinions. But I must say that when the opportunity comes to get near to most of these people and to get below the surface, their humility is definitely in place. Think about it. God would not allow them to be as exalted as they are without first passing the test of humility.

Are there exceptions? Certainly. There are false apostles. There are flaky prophets. There are greedy evangelists. There are deceitful pastors. There are self-serving teachers. Unfortunately, such individuals bring much discredit to the Body of Christ and they are blemishes on the kingdom of God. However, this book is not about them, except to warn them about the dangers of the passive verb: God *humbles* you.

God Steps In

If you choose to exalt yourself (active), then, sooner or later, you will be humbled (passive). The kind of people I mentioned in the last paragraph need to be acutely aware of a huge danger. If they are exalted because they have chosen to exalt themselves, they are in deep trouble. Since they have not chosen to humble themselves, God may step in at any moment and humble them Himself. When He does, trust me, it's too late! God is usually patient. Sometimes a proud individual may irritate us so much that we say, "God, when are You going to do something about this? This person should be taken off their platform and removed from ministry!" But God knows the timing better than we do, and fortunately when He intervenes, it is more often later than sooner.

God Still Restores

What do I mean that it is too late? I mean that if God has to step in and humble you, your ministry will never be the same. True, there is such a thing as restoration. If God humbles you, you can be restored, but you will regret it for the rest of your life. Your biography will have "before" and "after" chapters, and the "after" will not be so good.

King David is an excellent case in point. As I was collecting the material for this book, I happened to be reading 1 Samuel and 2 Samuel in my daily devotions. My Bible is a study Bible with introductory material before each book. I seldom read the introductions, but I did happen to read this one when I came to 2 Samuel, the story of David. It is in chapter 11 that David commits the sin with Bathsheba so that God has to step in and humble him through the prophet Nathan. The person who wrote the study Bible for 2 Samuel used this very revealing outline:

1. The Triumphs of David (Chapters 1-10)
2. The Transgressions of David (Chapter 11)
3. The Troubles of David (Chapters 12-24)[1]

This (unnamed) Bible scholar comments, "David's glory and fame fade, never to be the same again."[2] He confessed his sin and he was restored. He was a great king and many parents still name their sons after him. But if he had humbled himself in time, it would have been much better.

The case of Ananias and Sapphira in Acts 5 turned out even worse. In those days, many believers were selling their land and their homes and giving the proceeds to the Church. Ananias and Sapphira sold their property, and they had decided to keep some of the proceeds and donate some to the Church. But pride entered the picture. They chose to exalt themselves by proudly claiming that they were giving all to the Church just like some of the others were doing. In this case, God was not very patient. He immediately stepped in and took the extreme measure of humbling both of them by abruptly ending their lives!

Let me conclude this chapter by reiterating my main point: Being a humble person is your choice. If you make the right choice and apply it to your daily life, you will end up exalted! I believe that it is time to get serious about humility!

JOURNAL QUESTIONS

1. What are some ways we can humble ourselves?

2. What does it mean to be clothed with humility?

3. Why does God sometimes humble believers? What are some ways He humbles Christians, particularly leaders?

4. Why is it so difficult for leaders to be humble?

JOURNAL NOTES

Therefore, as God's chosen people, holy and dearly loved,
clothe yourselves with compassion, kindness, humility,
gentleness and patience.

COLOSSIANS 3:12, *NIV*

_____

_____

_____

_____

_____

_____

_____

_____

_____

HE GUIDES THE HUMBLE IN WHAT IS

RIGHT AND TEACHES THEM HIS WAY.

Psalm 25:9, *NIV*

THE TWO DIMENSIONS OF HUMILITY

Humility has two dimensions. One is our humility before God, and the other is our humility in relationships with other people. Let's call the first "vertical humility" and the second "horizontal humility."

FAITH WITH WORKS

This book is mostly about horizontal humility. But I must first stress the importance of vertical humility. Our humility before God is the indispensable foundation for our humility in personal relationships. Vertical humility is to horizontal humility as faith is to works. We do not gain faith by doing good works, but there is no such thing as genuine faith that does not produce good works.

That is why James writes: "Faith by itself, if it does not have works, is dead" (Jas. 2:17). There is such a thing as dead faith. But what is it that brings dead faith to life? Works! This is also true about humility. We can be humble before God, but if this does not play out in humility before other men and women around us, there is no life.

When it comes right down to it, the only measurable proof that we have real faith is our behavior. James goes on to say, "Show me your faith without your works, and I will show you my faith by my works" (Jas. 2:18). This is another way of saying that actions speak louder than words. We say that we are humble. Those are nice words, but the only way that anyone could sincerely evaluate whether this is true or false would be to observe whether we are humble in our dealings with others.

HUMILITY AND HOLINESS

Humility has many parallels to holiness. Andrew Murray associated them so closely to one another that he wrote, "The great test of whether the holiness we profess to seek or to attain is truth and life will be *whether it produces an increasing humility in us*" (emphasis his).[1]

Holiness is both internal and external. In my opinion, we live in an age that may be overly mercy driven. Because of this we hear statements such as "It may be true that Bob [or whomever] is not living a holy life, but his heart is right." Jesus would not accept such a remark. He said, "A tree is known by its fruit" (Matt. 12:33). The external validates the internal. "Out of the abundance of the heart the mouth speaks" (Matt. 12:34). How can we tell the difference between good people and bad people?

Jesus said, "A good man out of the good treasure of his heart brings forth good things, and an evil man out of the evil treasure brings forth evil things" (Matt. 12:35).

Holiness is also vertical and horizontal. On the vertical level we recognize our flawed humanity before the holiness of God. Isaiah saw a vision of two seraphim shouting, "Holy, holy, holy is the LORD of Hosts; the whole earth is full of His glory!" (Isa. 6:3). The holiness of God is so basic that, at least measured by the songs that we are currently singing in our churches, it draws much more attention than does the holiness of our own lives. One outcome of this is that, unfortunately, our generation suffers from a holiness deficiency.

A Holiness Deficiency?

Why do I suggest that we have a holiness deficiency? Christian author George Barna's research leads me to that conclusion. Holiness, at its roots, means to be set apart. Therefore, Christians who are presumably set apart to God (vertical), should also be set apart in their behavior from those around them who do not love and obey God (horizontal). But here is what Barna discovered:

> The Bible clearly states that true believers should be readily distinguished from nonbelievers by the way they live. Yet, the evidence undeniably suggests that most American Christians today do not live in a way that is quantifiably different from their non-Christian peers, in spite of the fact that they profess to believe in a set of principles that should clearly set them apart.[2]

The point I am trying to make is that humility, just like holiness, needs both dimensions, the vertical and the horizontal, in order to be complete. But, as far as our daily lives here on Earth are concerned, the horizontal matters most. Murray made the same point by quoting the Apostle John: "He who does not love his brother whom he has seen, how can he love God whom he has not seen?" (1 John 4:20). Murray wrote, "Our love to God will be found to be a delusion, except as its truth is proved in standing the test of daily life with our fellow-men. It is even so with humility. It is easy to think we humble ourselves before God. Yet, humility toward men will be the only sufficient proof that our humility before God is real."[3]

That is why the Apostle Peter wrote, "But as He who called you is holy [vertical], you also be holy in all your conduct [horizontal]" (1 Pet. 1:15).

A Fruit of the Spirit

The Bible instructs us to not be drunk with wine but to be filled with the Holy Spirit (see Eph. 5:18). Just about every believer deeply desires a full measure of the Holy Spirit, day by day and week by week. But how do we test whether we are, indeed, overflowing with the Holy Spirit? If we are, those around us will see the fruit of the Holy Spirit in how we conduct ourselves in our daily lives. What is the fruit? It is "love, joy, peace, longsuffering, kindness, goodness, faithfulness, gentleness, self-control" (Gal. 5:22-23). This is another reminder of the internal being validated by the external—faith *and* works.

I want to highlight the particular fruit of the Spirit that my *New King James Version* of the Holy Bible calls "gentleness." Other translations use the word "meekness"—which is rendered from the Greek *prayotes*. Prayotes is also one of the two New Testament root words for humility; the other is *tapeinophrosune*. It is, therefore, important to understand that humility is a fruit of the Spirit. If we stay filled with the Holy Spirit, more than likely we will be humble.

A Daily Dose

I believe that if we are to stay filled, we need to be refilled with the Holy Spirit each day. I know that some people disagree with this idea. I have heard some say: "I was filled with the Holy Spirit 14 years ago!" The implication is that their experience has lasted 14 years, and it probably will continue intact until they die.

But I base my differing point of view on the passage in Ephesians 5:18, in which being filled with the Holy Spirit is compared to getting drunk. Before I was saved, I was a habitual drunkard, which may give me an edge on interpreting this verse. During that forgettable period of my life, I learned that when I got drunk, the effect only lasted for one day. If I wanted to be drunk the next day, I had to fill up with alcohol all over again. The Bible declares that being filled with the Holy Spirit is like that.

> Being filled with the Holy Spirit each day is one way to attain the humility we desire.

Consequently, I recommend a new filling of the Holy Spirit each day. How does this happen? All we have to do is ask God to fill us with the Holy Spirit each morning. It is that simple. Jesus said, "If a son asks for bread from any father among you, will he give him a stone?" (Luke 11:11). This, naturally, was a rhetorical question. Therefore, Jesus goes on, "If you then, being evil, know how to give good gifts to your children, how much more will your heavenly Father give the Holy Spirit to those who ask Him?" (Luke 11:13).

Being filled with the Holy Spirit each day is one way to attain the humility we desire. When our heavenly Father gives us bread (the Holy Spirit) instead of a stone, this Holy Spirit will bear fruit throughout our lives. And a part of the fruit of the Spirit is humility, which is also called meekness and gentleness.

This is one place where the vertical and the horizontal come together. Asking the Father to fill us with the Holy Spirit is the vertical direction. When He does fill us, it can be seen by ourselves and by those around us as practical, everyday humility shown toward others. Vertical humility opens the door for horizontal humility.

Vertical Humility

Vertical humility is not that hard for us to understand and implement. The first and most important step is automatic for believers. No one has become a Christian without recognizing these humbling facts:

- I am a creature standing before God, the Creator.
- I have a human nature and God has a divine nature.
- I am a sinner and God is completely pure.

Once we recognize these truths and hear that Jesus died for our sins and, in faith, humble ourselves before God by confessing our sins and asking Him to forgive us through the blood of Jesus, we are born again by the Holy Spirit. Old things are passed away and we are new creatures in Christ Jesus. Everyone who is an authentic Christian identifies with and has gone through this process, in one way or another, and they have begun their Christian walk with vertical humility.

Nothingness and Helplessness

Here is the way that Andrew Murray expressed it: "We need only think for a moment what faith is. Is it not the confession of nothingness and helplessness, the surrender and the waiting to let God work? Is it not in itself the most humbling thing there can be—the acceptance of our place as dependents, who can claim or get or do nothing but what grace bestows?"[4] It could not be said any better!

Once we are born again, we quickly discover that another aspect of vertical humility provides us the pattern for the rest of our spiritual journey. The Bible declares, "Let this mind be in you which was also in Christ Jesus" (Phil. 2:5). What does "this mind" refer to? "[Jesus] humbled Himself" (Phil. 2:8). Even though He was God, He agreed to take on and live His life on Earth through a human nature, even going so far as to die a human death on the cross. Humility was at the core of Jesus' life and ministry, and we must have this same mind-set if we are going to be everything that God wants us to be.

Jesus' Teachings on Humility

The best way to understand what this mind-set of Jesus actually implies for us is to study the words of Jesus Himself. Murray's book is very convincing on this and on other aspects of vertical humility. By contrast, my book deals mostly with our horizontal humility. But before I get to that, I am going to borrow Murray's list of what he considers the nine most important teachings of Jesus on humility. Murray adds his comments for each item, but I am just going to list the teachings and the Bible reference:

1. Blessed are the poor in spirit, for theirs is the kingdom of heaven. . . . Blessed are the meek [humble], for they shall inherit the earth (Matt. 5:3-5).
2. Learn from Me, for I am gentle [meek, humble] and lowly in heart, and you will find rest for your souls (Matt. 11:29).
3. Whoever humbles himself as this little child is the greatest in the kingdom of heaven (Matt. 18:4).
4. Whoever desires to become great among you, let him be your servant. And whoever desires to be first among you, let him be your slave (Matt. 20:26-27).

5. He who is greatest among you shall be your servant (Matt. 23:11).
6. For whoever exalts himself will be humbled, and he who humbles himself will be exalted (Luke 14:11).
7. Everyone who exalts himself will be humbled, and he who humbles himself will be exalted (Luke 18:14).
8. If I then, your Lord and Teacher, have washed your feet, you also ought to wash one another's feet (John 13:14).
9. He who is greatest among you, let him be as the younger, and he who governs as he who serves.... I am among you as the One who serves (Luke 22:26-27).[5]

Onward to Horizontal Humility

Having the mind of Jesus, according to the terminology I am using in this book, fulfills the need to begin with vertical humility and internal humility. How this actually plays out in daily life with horizontal and external humility is what I endeavor to explain in practical detail in the following chapters.

Humility has two dimensions. If the first is in place—our humility before God—then we are ready to move into the second—how we relate to other people.

JOURNAL QUESTIONS

1. How will being filled with the Holy Spirit each day produce greater humility in your life?

2. What is the difference between humility before man and humility before God? Why is it important to achieve both?

3. List the ways that Jesus humbled Himself.

4. List some ways that we can humble ourselves as little children, as we are instructed to do in Matthew 18:4.

JOURNAL NOTES

Therefore whoever humbles himself as this little child
is the greatest in the kingdom of heaven.

MATTHEW 18:4

NOW THE MAN MOSES WAS
VERY HUMBLE, MORE THAN ALL
MEN WHO WERE ON THE FACE
OF THE EARTH.

Numbers 12:3

WHAT EXACTLY IS HUMILITY?

It is important to recognize true humility when you see it. Nothing helps more to recognize true humility than to know what phony, or counterfeit, humility looks like. In this chapter, I want to clarify those distinctions.

A good way to begin the process of understanding true humility is to take a close look at the life of a person that the Bible characterizes as humble. I have found it helpful, in this regard, to look to Moses as a good example of humbleness.

MOSES' HUMILITY

Moses is not only one of the most highly regarded biblical personalities, but he has also gone down in history as one of the outstanding leaders of the human race. Very few people would deny Moses that distinction. He was a powerful leader and an incomparable role model for people of all religions. Yet, according to Numbers 12:3, "The man Moses was very humble, more than all men who were on the face of the earth."

This means that Moses was the humblest man in the world at that time. Some Bible translators use the word "meekest" instead of "humblest" to render the Hebrew 'anaw. So in Moses we have a combination of the most powerful leader in the world and the humblest individual. This fits well with what Jesus would say centuries later: "He who humbles himself will be exalted" (Matt. 23:12).

Miriam Exalted

In Numbers 12, Moses' sister, Miriam, suddenly wanted to re-place Moses as the leader of the children of Israel. She recruited Aaron and attempted a coup. Moses, however, rose to the occasion and endured the attacks and criticism with dignity and integrity. It was a serious enough matter to cause God to inter-vene personally. He told Miriam and Aaron directly that Moses was His appointed and anointed leader. Miriam had exalted her-self, and God, true to His nature, responded by humbling her. He punished Miriam, apparently the ringleader of the rebellion, with an instant case of leprosy. Moses again showed his true character when he prayed for Miriam to be healed. God, as we know, miraculously healed her. However, while Miriam had been restored, she was never the same. The only notation we read about Miriam after that incident is that she died and was buried (see Num. 20:1).

Let me repeat what I wrote in chapter 1: When God has to step in and humble you, it is too late! It is much better to hum-ble yourself as a part of your ongoing lifestyle, following the example of Moses.

THE KNOWLEDGE OF OUR HUMILITY

Did you ever consider that the author of the famous statement that Moses was more humble than anyone else on Earth was Moses himself? Moses wrote the first five books of the Bible, Numbers being the third. If you have not thought of it before, the idea usually comes as a bit of a shock. In fact, it has shocked some Bible scholars so much that they hypothesize that a later editor of Numbers must have inserted the comment. In their minds, Moses could not have been egotistical enough to declare himself to be humble. If he had, such a statement would effectively nullify his humility. This might remind us of the clergy joke I wrote about earlier: the satirical book title *Humility and How I Attained It!*

> The author of the famous statement that Moses was more humble than anyone else on Earth was Moses himself!

Let's think about this for a moment. I believe it is quite a significant issue. Can a truly humble person recognize that he or she is humble and verbalize it to others? Why not? Consider biblical scholar A. A. MacRae's comment on Moses:

> Faults are not hidden or glossed over, nor is there any false modesty about presenting good points exactly as they were. Writing under the inspiration of the Holy Spirit, Moses did not hesitate to record his own sins and weaknesses, using the clearest language. It would be contrary to the remarkable objectivity of the Bible if he did not also record his strongest point: his meekness.[1]

This thought made me ask myself the question, *What credentials do I have to write a whole book about humility?* Can someone write a book on humility if he or she is not humble? It is really not such a difficult question. Can someone write a book on investing in the stock market if they are in bankruptcy? Can someone write a book on dieting if they are obese and have never successfully dieted? Can someone write a book on how to raise children whose kids have grown up to be troublemakers and are in jail? In this vein, it has occurred to me that I should probably not attempt to write a book on humility if I myself am not humble and if I cannot serve as a role model. True, I am not overly accustomed to actually saying that I am humble, and that makes this paragraph a rather difficult one to write. I would not be surprised, nor would I be upset, if some readers found themselves taking offense at this point.

Biblical Examples

I do have biblical examples to support my point. As I have already noted, Moses is one clear case. Jesus and Paul are others—each of them also characterized themselves as humble.

Jesus said, "I am gentle and lowly in heart" (Matt. 11:29). The word "gentle" in the *New King James Version* is translated "meek" in some other versions. It is related to the Greek word "prayotes," which I mentioned in the last chapter. In fact, the *New Living Translation* renders the statement: "I am humble and gentle." Jesus, I realize, is the second person of the Trinity and, thus, God Himself, but we still can follow His example. We should also be able to say "I am humble and gentle," especially since both characteristics are listed in Galatians 5 as fruit of the Holy Spirit.

Paul, however, was a human being just as we are. In 2 Corinthians, the epistle in which he most assuredly displayed his credentials as an apostle, Paul also wrote, "I, Paul, myself am pleading with you by the meekness and gentleness of Christ—who in presence am lowly among you" (2 Cor. 10:1). The word "meekness" that is used here also comes from the Greek word "prayotes," the word for humility. Paul, apparently, had no problem in personally identifying with Jesus' assertion that He was humble. Therefore, while Paul was exalted by God as an apostle, he also recognized that one reason that God had seen fit to do this was because he (Paul) had chosen to humble himself.

THE REALITY OF
FALSE HUMILITY

Before anyone can come to the conclusion that he or she is humble, it would help to know what kind of behavior falls within the bounds of humility, and what kind is outside the bounds. For the sake of clarity, I will split it into two categories:

- False humility
- Counterfeit, or phony, humility

Even though these two concepts are virtually synonymous, I feel it is good to separate them because the Bible is very specific on the meaning of "false humility." In fact, false humility only appears in one chapter of Bible—Colossians 2, where it comes up twice:

Let no one cheat you of your reward, taking delight in *false humility* (Col. 2:18, emphasis added).

These things indeed have an appearance of wisdom in self-imposed religion, *false humility*, and neglect of the body (Col. 2:23, emphasis added).

These two references to false humility are five verses apart. What is between the two of them? Four verses on legalism. In other words, the biblical definition of false humility is "legalism." Here is a part of the text:

> Therefore, if you died with Christ from the basic principles of the world, why, as though living in the world, do you subject yourselves to regulations—"do not touch, do not taste, do not handle," which all concern things which perish with the using—according to the commandments and doctrines of men? (Col. 2:20-22).

What Is Legalism?

What do I mean by "legalism"? I looked for an answer to that question in several books where the authors write about legalism. They all describe it in some detail, but, surprisingly, none of them offered a definition. So here is my attempt at a definition of legalism: Legalism is gauging conduct by strict adherence to a set of rules, with emphasis on the letter rather than on the spirit of the rules, accompanied by moral condemnation of those who choose not to conform.

Legalism is based upon external constraints and the punishments handed out to those who violate laws. Grace is based upon internal constraints. We need both. Laws define and limit how we should behave according to man's code of conduct. God's grace gives us the freedom to develop the kind of character that causes us to behave as we should in His mercy. Big difference!

Dress-Code Humility

This legalism plays itself out in many ways. Some people decide that their rules will involve a dress code. They reason that people will see that they are humble if they do not wear makeup or jewelry. My sign of humility is preaching in jeans and an open shirt instead of a tie and a suit. I let my beard grow without trimming it and I hardly ever comb my hair. I do not believe in buying expensive clothes or in keeping up with the latest fashions.

Legalism can apply to other lifestyle issues, too. My house is more modest than the lavish one that you live in. Look! I have an older model car than you. You live in a gated community? What kind of a testimony is that? I live in an integrated neighborhood and most of my neighbors belong to nonwhite ethnic groups.

Fasting Humility

Here is another example: I have noticed that a subtle kind of legalism may have developed along with the growing popularity of fasting. Even as few as 10 years ago, very few Christians fasted. Not so today. Fasting has become the "in thing." Some people consider fasting to be a major sign of humility. They associate it with 2 Chronicles 7:14, which starts with these words: "If my people will humble themselves." For some people, nothing is presumed to exhibit the biblical mandate to humble themselves more than fasting.

Their conversation might sound like this: "You only fasted three days? I fasted 40 days!" Such mind-sets could cross the boundary into legalism. In order to accomplish longer fasts, some have invented the "blender fast." That means that while you fast, you can drink anything that you can produce in your blender. I have heard of big-time fasters exchanging blender recipes! In fact, one Christian leader reportedly gained weight during a 40-day fast! A church bulletin that came to my attention carried a notice promoting a National Prayer and Fasting Conference. It added, "The cost for attending the Fasting and Prayer Conference includes meals!"

So much for legalism! The Bible plainly calls it false humility.

COUNTERFEIT, OR PHONY, HUMILITY

Many other subtle and equally deceptive things often parade as signs of humility. Christian writer John Bevere, for example, quotes the apostle Paul as saying, "For I am the least of the apostles, who am not worthy to be called an apostle" (1 Cor. 15:9). Bevere's comment: "Counterfeit humility knows how to use politically correct words in order to appear humble, yet there is no lowliness of heart or mind." This is a real danger. But he adds, "When Paul said he was the bottom of the barrel of the apostles, it wasn't politically correct jargon, but rather true humility."[2]

Here is a distinction that we would do well to keep in mind. False humility may take on forms other than legalism, but Bevere's phrase, "counterfeit humility," provides a helpful distinction.

> The dictionary defines humble as "not proud or arrogant; modest; *to be humble although successful.*"

Other common badges of counterfeit, or phony, humility might include being poor, belittling yourself, being chronically ill, weakness, allowing others to walk all over you, seeing yourself as a "worm" (as the line in Charles Wesley's hymn: "such a worm as I," although Wesley himself did not teach "worm theology") and having a "doormat" mentality, shyness. I have noticed that some misdirected authors apparently think it is humble not to include a byline on their manuscripts or articles. They fail to realize that communication is highly personal and that readers need to know who is communicating to them. Anonymous authors have the wrong idea about humility.

The dictionary defines humble as "not proud or arrogant; modest; *to be humble although successful.*"[3] This is what we really should aim for. "Successful" in this definition is closely related to what the Bible calls "exalted." Sooner or later, the person who is truly humble will be successful or exalted. The two must not be seen as opposites. In fact, Jesus said, "Blessed are the meek [humble], for they shall inherit the earth" (Matt. 5:5). Most people would consider "inheriting the earth" a success.

Humility Is Not Perfection

If we recognize humility for what it is and admit that we really are humble, this in no way implies that we are perfect. God requires us to be humble, just as He requires us to be holy, but He has never required, or even expected, us to be perfect.

Some people have not understood this important distinction because they remember what Jesus said: "Therefore you shall be perfect, just as your Father in heaven is perfect" (Matt. 5:48). This is a classic translation problem. "Perfect" in this verse comes from the Greek *teleios*. The meaning of teleios is not a flawless moral nature but maturity. What Jesus was saying is that we are supposed to live up to everything that God wants us to be.

The problem is that almost all English translations render teleios as "perfect" and that can throw us off track at this point. The only translation I found that really brings out the meaning is Eugene Peterson's *The Message*, which declares, "In a word, what I'm saying is, Grow up. You're kingdom subjects. Now live like it. Live out your God-created identity. Live generously and graciously toward others, the way God lives toward you." Once we understand this, we know how we can be humble without at the same time being perfect.

Humility Is Not Absolute

We should not, therefore, think of humility or being humble as absolutes. It is not that you are either humble or you are not.

Humility is not similar to being pregnant. We cannot say that one pregnant woman is more pregnant than another. Humility, on the other hand, is a range. Not all humble people are equal. They are more like National Football League quarterbacks. There are dozens of quarterbacks in the NFL, and every single one of them is a good quarterback or they would not be where they are. But they are not all equal. Some are better quarterbacks than others.

Exalted Christian leaders whom I know are, likewise, not equally humble. But they have passed the tests and met God's basic standards. Truly humble people, for the most part, desire to be more humble next year than this year. Growing in humility is a lifelong process. I pray that this book will not only help some start on the road to humility but also that it will be a tool to help all of us continue to grow.

JOURNAL QUESTIONS

1. How could Moses (or anyone) declare he was humble and, at the same time, remain humble?

2. What are some traits of false or counterfeit humility in the Church and in Christians today?

3. List some of the forms of false or counterfeit humility in your own life, past or present.

4. What have been the tests of humility in your life? Have you passed them?

JOURNAL NOTES

Do not let anyone who delights in false humility and
the worship of angels disqualify you for the prize. Such a person
goes into great detail about what he has seen, and his unspiritual
mind puffs him up with idle notions.

COLOSSIANS 2:18, *NIV*

_____

_____

_____

_____

_____

_____

_____

_____

_____

_____

_____

_____

_____

_____

_____

_____

_____

_____

_____

_____

_____

_____

_____

THEREFORE LAY ASIDE ALL FILTHINESS

AND OVERFLOW OF WICKEDNESS, AND

RECEIVE WITH MEEKNESS THE

IMPLANTED WORD, WHICH IS ABLE TO

SAVE YOUR SOULS.

James 1:21

IT IS YOUR DECISION!

To be humble or not to be humble is a choice each of us makes. I base this rather blunt thought on the foundational Scripture for this book: "Whoever exalts himself will be humbled, and he who humbles himself will be exalted" (Matt. 23:12). This quote from Jesus is built around action verbs. What you finally achieve in your life will clearly depend on the decisions you make now, and the actions you take to implement those decisions. Jesus would not have put it this way unless He knew that you personally had the power to decide to humble yourself or to exalt yourself.

THE RIGHT CHOICE

How, then, do you make the right decision? It is essentially a matter of how you *think*. Look at these two well-known verses from Romans 12:

Do not be conformed to this world, but be transformed by the renewing of your mind, that you may prove what is that good and acceptable and perfect will of God. For I say, through the grace given to me, to everyone who is among you, not to think of himself more highly than he ought to think, but to think soberly, as God has dealt to each one a measure of faith (vv. 2-3).

There are two operative phrases in this Scripture, one in each verse:

- Verse 2: "The renewing of your mind." If we renew our minds, we can be transformed. This frees us to do God's will. Renewing our minds is a decision for each of us to make. Our minds have to do with how we think. This is not a matter of our *hearts*; it is a matter of our *minds*.
- Verse 3: "Think soberly of yourself." This means that we are supposed to be very clear in our own self-perception as to exactly who God has created each of us to be. We are not a random happenstance on this Earth. God has designed each of us for a specific purpose, and He desires to fulfill this purpose.

Apply the Law of the Lid

Former pastor and church-planting expert John Maxwell has written a book titled *The 21 Irrefutable Laws of Leadership*. He calls the first law "The Law of the Lid." This law applies to each of us in many ways. Maxwell's application is that a person's effectiveness is limited (the "lid") by their leadership ability. Among other things, he encourages them to read the rest of his book in order to increase their leadership skills and thereby raise their level of effectiveness. This is important because very few people, including leaders, are at a place where they cannot improve their skills—they just need to muster their desire to grow.

The Law of the Lid also relates to the specific purpose for which God has created you. God did not create everyone the same. It would not be good *thinking* to suppose that the only reason someone else is more effective in leadership or whatever form of ministry is solely because that person listened to more tapes or read more books on the subject. Each person's divine lid is different. Not everyone on a World Series-quality baseball team bats .300, even though everyone on the team wants to. Each one of us has our own God-determined level of potential, and "thinking soberly" about what it really is helps enormously in reaching that potential. When we do that, we are then in a position to make our best possible contribution to the team as a whole.

Know When You Are Exalted

How can you tell if you have been exalted? You have been exalted if you reach that very top level of potential for which God has designed you. You will not know what your potential is if you make the mistake of comparing yourself unfavorably to other people whom God has designed differently. You will only know your potential if you renew your mind and think soberly of *yourself*. If you use others as your measuring stick, it will load you down with heaps of unwarranted frustration. On the other hand, by thinking soberly you will be able to put your personal humility in the proper perspective. As you are taking the trip of humility, this will help you to know when you have arrived.

> You have been exalted if you reach that very top level of potential for which God has designed you.

In his book *So I'm Not Perfect: A Psychology of Humility*, psychotherapist Robert Furey uses the Alcoholics Anonymous motto to illustrate this point. A.A., an organization that stresses genuine humility, has adopted this prayer:

> *God, grant me the serenity [humility] to accept the things*
> *I cannot change, courage to change the things I can and*
> *wisdom to know the difference.*

Furey comments:

> Humility is a virtue which, as a culture, we are trying to struggle without. The development of an identity is too often a fight for superiority and a flight from inferiority. We cannot attain happiness, however, until we accept the things about ourselves which we cannot change.[1]

For example, God may have designed "Joe" to be a cell group leader. If Joe is one of the best cell group leaders in the county, he has definitely been exalted! You should never think that you cannot be exalted unless you become a senior pastor, much less a megachurch pastor. God has designed very few individuals to be senior pastors. Your exaltation may be serving as an usher who counts the offering, a fifth-grade Sunday School teacher, one who visits the hospitals and prays for the sick or a successful businessperson who finances important ministries.

How does all this relate to humility? Only if you decide to be humble in recognizing, understanding and carrying out God's purpose for your own life will you then be exalted and achieve the top potential of whatever your divine assignment happens to be.

GOOD AND BAD DECISIONS

I want to use both biblical and current-day figures as examples. I will include people who have made decisions to humble themselves and people who have made decisions to exalt themselves.

Good Decision: King Josiah

King Josiah is a good example of how humility enables a person to reach his or her potential. When Josiah became king, idolatry had penetrated every stratum of society in Judah. Josiah did the right thing and he inquired of the Lord. He discovered through the prophet Huldah that God had decided to "bring calamity on this place and on its inhabitants" (2 Kings 22:16) because they were worshiping other gods. But the Lord also told Josiah that he would have peace during his own reign. The Lord said, "Your eyes shall not see all the calamity which I will bring on this place" (2 Kings 22:20). Why would God make this exception? He said to Josiah, "Because your heart was tender, and you *humbled* yourself" (2 Kings 22:19, emphasis added).

Josiah was exalted. How exalted? The Bible records, "Now before him there was no king like him . . . nor after him did any arise like him" (2 Kings 23:25). That is about as high as you can go in fulfilling God's purpose for your life! He ended up exalted because he was humble.

Good Decision: John Stott

A current-day role model for humility is John Stott of England.

I am choosing Stott because he and I have known each other for 30 years. Even before I met him, I had frequently said, "I want to be like John Stott when I grow up." I still do! Few Christian leaders have gained as much admiration and respect from such a broad spectrum in the evangelical community as has John Stott.

How did Stott arrive at such an enviable position? John Yates, who served for several years as Stott's study assistant, can answer this question better than most. In a recent article, Yates asserts that "a key characteristic of John Stott [is] his disarming humility."[2]

Yates tells the story of his first assignment: critiquing and editing a 10-page handwritten John Stott manuscript. More than a little nervous and apprehensive, Yates conscientiously marked the manuscript quite heavily and returned it. Yates reports that the next day "the [manuscript] had been rewritten—and every single suggestion employed. Britain's world-renowned, 75-year-old writer and teacher had consented to every piece of advice from a recent college graduate on his first day of work."[3]

I am definitely not the only one who wants to be like Stott when I grow up. But the reason he has become such an enviable role model is that at an early age Stott decided to humble himself. He never sought exaltation, but he received it because he chose humility and passed the tests during the course of his career.

Bad Decision: King Uzziah

Uzziah, like Josiah, was one of the kings of Judah who belonged to the select group of those who "did what was right in the sight of the LORD" (2 Chron. 26:4). God honored Uzziah's faith by making him an awesome warrior whose "fame spread as far as the entrance of Egypt, for he became exceedingly strong" (2 Chron. 26:8). He was a good man and one of the greatest heroes of his generation.

But Uzziah made a huge mistake by deciding to exalt himself. "When he was strong his heart was lifted up to his destruction" (2 Chron. 26:16). How did he do it? In those days, only the priests were allowed to go into the Temple and burn incense to the Lord. But Uzziah decided that if the priests could do it, so could he. Since he was a great king, he decided that he did not have to humble himself and admit that the priests could do something that he could not do. So Uzziah, against the warnings of the priests, made the bad decision to go into the sanctuary and burn incense. What was the result? God had to step in and humble the king. God struck him with leprosy, and while he was still king, he was forced to live isolated in quarantine for the rest of his life!

Bad Decision: William Branham

A huge wave of evangelism swept into the Church after World War II. But back in the late 1940s and early 1950s the wall between evangelicals and Pentecostals was so high that the Holy Spirit had to speak separately to both sectors. The two who became best known for hearing what the Spirit was saying and taking leadership of the new movement of evangelism were Billy Graham of the evangelicals and William Branham of the Pentecostals.

When we recently moved into the twenty-first century, numerous periodicals published lists of the most influential people of the preceding century. Billy Graham's name was on virtually every list. But William Branham's name was on none. William who? Today, only a few well-informed old-timers can tell you who Branham was. He is all but forgotten.

This is very odd, because for two decades, week by week, meeting by meeting, Branham's meetings were much larger than Graham's. Branham would deliver prophecies. Seemingly at will, he would, with pinpoint accuracy, call out people's names, family members, Social Security numbers and other private information. After his meetings there would be huge piles of crutches and rows of empty wheelchairs left by people who had been healed—something unseen at Billy Graham's meetings. Message for message, many more people found the road to heaven through Branham than through Graham.

But now we ask, "William who?" What happened?

I am indebted to research done by Eddie Hyatt for the answer to this crucial question. Before I quote from him, however, it is important to know that Gordon Lindsay is an important player in the story. Lindsay was the editor of *The Voice of Healing* magazine. (He later founded Christ for the Nations Institute in Dallas, Texas, to this day one of the finest schools in the world for training Christian leaders. He is deceased, but his widow, Freda, carries on strongly.) As this story unfolds, Lindsay was serving as the campaign manager for William Branham.

Here are some extremely revealing paragraphs from Eddie Hyatt's research:

> When the time came for Branham to preach in the evening services, Lindsay would introduce him in a low-key manner while at the same time acknowledging that God was using him in a remarkable way. Once, when Lindsay was away, a brother B— introduced Branham. His flowery introduction was filled with glowing accolades, and he referred to Branham as a special end-time prophet of God. When Lindsay returned, Branham said, "Brother Lindsay, I would like for Brother B— to introduce me from now on."
>
> Branham then began to surround himself with individuals who fed his ego with ideas about being a special end-time prophet of God. Lindsay sought to warn him, but his advice was not heeded, and he later withdrew from involvement in Branham's ministry.
>
> This was the beginning of a sad departure from the simple humility in which Branham's ministry had begun. He eventually came to believe that he was the fulfillment

of the promise of God in Malachi 4:5 which says, "I will send you Elijah the prophet before the coming of the great and dreadful day of the Lord." Branham believed that in the same way John the Baptist fulfilled this Scripture before the first coming of Christ, that he was the fulfillment of the same Scripture before the second coming of Christ. He believed that he was, in reality, Elijah preparing the way for the coming of Christ.[4]

William Branham was a good man, just like Uzziah. He started in humility and God exalted him. But God's exaltation was not enough. Branham made the unwise decision to exalt himself, and he arrived at that point where God had to step in and humble him. In this case it definitely was too late for Branham. Here is what happened:

[In 1965], Lindsay received a call from out of state asking him to come and pray for Branham who had been in a car accident and was in serious condition. Because of his previous experiences Lindsay felt that he was to leave the situation completely in the hands of God, and so he did not go. Branham died shortly thereafter, and it was reported that his head was swollen to twice its normal size from the injuries of the impact.[5]

William who?

YOUR DECISION

In light of these examples, what will your decision be? I want my decision to be like those of King Josiah and John Stott, not like those of King Uzziah and William Branham. And I am sure that you desire the same thing!

JOURNAL QUESTIONS

1. How does your thought life directly affect your level of humility?

2. List some examples from your life and from the lives of others where good decisions have been made regarding humility. Write down the decisions and how making the right decisions resulted in your being exalted.

3. List some examples from your life and from the lives of others where bad decisions have been made regarding humility. Write down the decisions that were made and the results of those decisions. Why were they bad decisions? What could you have done differently to make them good decisions?

4. What challenges do you face in your life right now where you can make good decisions about humility?

JOURNAL NOTES

Before destruction the heart of man is haughty,
but humility goes before honor.

PROVERBS 18:12, *NASB*

_____

_____

_____

_____

_____

_____

_____

_____

_____

WHEN PRIDE COMES,

THEN COMES SHAME; BUT WITH THE

HUMBLE IS WISDOM.

Proverbs 11:2

FIVE SIGNPOSTS ALONG THE ROAD TO PRIDE

Pride is the opposite of humility. First Peter 5:5 instructs us to be "clothed with humility." The same verse goes on to say, "for God resists the proud, but gives grace to the humble." The last thing that any Christian would want is for God to resist or stand against us. Therefore, we must, at all costs, avoid pride.

DEFINING PRIDE

The dictionary defines "pride" as "a high or inordinate opinion of one's own dignity, importance, merit, or superiority, whether as cherished in the mind or as displayed in bearing, conduct, etc."[1]

Some words that describe facets of pride are "arrogance," "haugh-tiness," "vainglory," "conceit," "egotism," "stuck-up," "vanity" and "self-admiration."

Pride always seems to be lurking around the corner. Andrew Murray wrote:

> Devilish pride creeps in almost everywhere. . . . Think about how all the lack of love, the indifference to the needs, feelings and weaknesses of others, the sharp and hasty judgments and utterances so often excused by our cries of being upright and honest, the manifestations of temper and irritation, the bitterness and estrangement, have their root in pride. Pride seeks only itself.[2]

Pride and Self-Esteem

I like Murray's phrase "devilish pride." However, do not confuse this kind of sinful loftiness for healthy self-esteem. Self-esteem is thinking soberly of ourselves and realizing that we are what God made us to be (see Rom. 12:3). Some people, in fact, label healthy self-esteem as a benign sort of pride. Psychologist Robert Furey concluded, "Humility and pride compose a dialectic; each concept gives the other meaning. Without humility, pride becomes arrogance and conceit. Without pride [self-esteem], humility becomes passivity and complacency."[3]

A Bad Road

The road to arrogant and ungodly pride is a bad road. Do not take it. If you find yourself following any of the five signposts listed in this chapter, please turn around. Renew your mind before it is too late. God is characterized by tolerance and patience—to a point. But if you pass that point, He may well decide to step in and humble you. If He ever does, it promises to be a very sad day!

The best way to avoid this is to recognize the symptoms of pride as soon as they begin to appear. That is why it is essential to become familiar with these signposts of approaching pride.

Tests of Youth

As a general rule, the younger a person is, the greater the temptations of pride. There are exceptions, of course, but not too many. It is important to understand that God is the only one who exalts a person into authentic Christian leadership, whatever form a particular exaltation might take. God knows very well that the higher a person finds himself in Christian leadership, the greater damage to the kingdom of God pride could cause. Consequently, before He allows a person to reach the higher levels, He makes sure that the person has passed the tests of pride at a young age.

Among the many requirements for Christian leadership, 1 Timothy 3:6 notes that the leader must not be a "novice"— a term that would generally apply to a younger person. Why? "Lest being puffed up with pride, he fall into the same condemnation as the devil." Pride can and very easily does blindside younger Christians.

Of course, pride can also blindside more mature leaders, such as it did with William Branham—but this does not occur as easily. The reason is that those to whom God has entrusted leadership roles have for the most part already come to terms with pride. They have fought many battles, and they have won more than they have lost. They may still bear scars, but they have passed the tests.

As I have already noted, partly as a result of my advanced age, I have the privilege of enjoying quite close relationships with a number of outstanding Christian leaders. Frequently when we get together we will comment to one another, "We have nothing to prove!" And while that may be the case, every one of us can still clearly remember back to those days when we *did* have something to prove! That was in our younger days when we began to learn how to read the signposts along the road to pride and how to turn away from them.

The Holy Spirit

How do we recognize these signposts? An essential starting point is to be filled constantly with the Holy Spirit. A vital ministry of the Holy Spirit in us is to convince us of sin, righteousness and judgment (see John 16:8). One of the things I personally have learned to do is to ask God for several things at the beginning of each and every day. Among many other things, I always specifically ask Him to keep me from the temptation of pride and to fill me with His Holy Spirit—and I believe that He answers my prayer. Consequently, when a pride issue appears, I know it for what it is and I can make my decision not to go there. This gives me the advantage of not being blindsided—at least not too often.

For example, two notable things related to pride happened to me in 2000. The first was at the beginning of the year when the book *Praying for the World's 365 Most Influential People* was released. The editors included me in that book. When I received my copy, even though I had known beforehand that it was coming out, I am ashamed to say that I succumbed to a very serious case of pride. (I will give more details about that later in this chapter.) By contrast, in the same year a magazine was published that featured my picture on the front cover. Even though this was the first time such a thing had happened to me, it did not cause any pride.

My different responses to these two incidents, naturally raises a question. How do I know that one caused pride while the other did not? Very simple: Through it all I was filled with the

Holy Spirit. In one case the Holy Spirit convicted me severely of pride; in the other He did not.

SIGNPOST 1: YEARNING FOR PRAISE AND HUMAN ACCOLADES

Being the object of praise does not necessarily cause pride. But *yearning* for praise can very rapidly lead to pride. One way to avoid this is to acknowledge praise but not to enjoy it too much. It helps if we can develop a mind set that will, at least initially, attribute most praise to either a formality of protocol or to a good-hearted effort on the part of someone to make you like them or to set you up for a favor. For example, pastors who believe everything that parishioners tell them as they shake hands at the church door after a Sunday sermon are living with something other than a realistic mind-set.

When you allow yourself to receive an emotional high from praise, it can be addictive. It can open the door for you to say to yourself, *I'm really good! I deserve this praise! I have an appetite for more of it!*

This is exactly what happened to William Branham, as we saw in the last chapter. If only Branham had regarded Brother B——'s declaration—that he was some kind of an end-time prophet preparing the way for the second coming of Christ—as a kindly but misguided effort to gain Branham's favor, little harm would have been done. Again, if he had heeded Gordon Lindsay's warnings against imagining that he was Elijah himself, Branham might have gotten as much respect as Billy Graham. But, no, Branham instead began to yearn for more and more praise and human accolades. He yielded to pride, which then escalated to the extent that God had to step in and humble him.

Praise and Accolades

What concrete steps can we take to avoid opening doors to pride through human praise? I have some specific suggestions. However, I am careful to call them suggestions right up front, because when we try to apply them to real life, it is all too easy to cross the line into legalism and, thereby, engage in false humility, as I explained in chapter 3. A suggestion is not by any means to be seen as a law. Furthermore, I want to make it clear that I am only giving my personal opinion on these matters. I fully realize that others may have different opinions and they, in fact, might be wiser and closer to the truth and more humble than I. Still, as the author of this book, I feel the obligation to offer some ideas.

One opinion has to do with personal trophy rooms. As people rise in Christian leadership, on certain occasions they might be presented with a physical object, often inscribed, praising them for certain accomplishments. What do these Christian leaders do with these objects? I can see how it might be appropriate for military officers to pin medals on their uniform or for professional athletes to exhibit their trophies and souvenir baseballs or footballs in a display case. A golfer might want to frame a scorecard highlighting a hole-in-one. But Christian leaders showing their collection of awards? In my opinion these articles should be placed in the attic for some grandchild to discover on an exploratory trip there.

Ego Walls

A related potential magnet of pride is what some people have called "ego walls." It begins when a person has his first picture taken with a Christian celebrity—a president, a media personality, a sports hero or someone like that. He frames the picture and hangs it on the wall. Then he begins to yearn for other celebrity photographs to hang there with it—before long his ego wall is born. This ego wall is usually located where visitors to his office or home are sure to see it. These pictures, understandably, have a sentimental value. It is fun for him to remember those high points of life. But in my opinion these photographs would do better in an album tucked into some shelf, not displayed on a wall.

Solicited Praise

I frequently get requests for letters of praise or videotapes congratulating leaders who are celebrating anniversaries of ordination, pastoring a certain church or founding a ministry. This is a game that I personally do not like to play because I see a big difference between *solicited* praise and *unsolicited* praise. True, these highlight events featuring solicited praise are typically initiated by friends, board members, family or staff—not by the leaders themselves. However, I have made my opinion known to my own friends, board members, staff and family that I do not want them to solicit praise for me as long as I live. I remarked to one staff member that such things should be reserved for funerals. She replied, "But then you wouldn't be able to hear them!" That was precisely my point—I do not ever want to hear the kind of accolades that can become an entry point for pride.

> While the use of titles can be important, even essential in some cultures, in our American culture the lust for titles can be a symptom of pride.

While the use of titles can be important, even essential, in some cultures, such as those in parts of Asia, in our American culture the lust for titles can be a symptom of pride. Some people hold titles as a prized possession, and they are a bit offended when the desired term—perhaps "doctor," "bishop," "pastor" or "apostle"—is not used. This is often the case among individuals who are insecure and who attempt, through insisting on titles, to build a self-assuring case of superiority.

Billy Graham, for example, requires that his team members refer to him as "Mr. Graham," regardless of how others may choose to address him. With all his fame, he refuses to play the title game. Ralph and Gretchen Mahoney, who bring this up in *World MAP Digest*, extend the thought: "Others may hang honorifics on you. You can't control that, but you can reject prideful seeking of honor. You can refuse to pursue fame and glory as your goal and god."[4]

SIGNPOST 2: KEEPING SCORE

What do I mean by "keeping score"? I mean developing a system under which we can calculate how many self-defined, prestige-loaded "points" we have accumulated. Once we begin doing this, we then begin to calculate how many points others *don't* have. The more people we find with fewer points than we have, the better we feel. Do this often enough, and we can become intoxicated with superiority!

I am sorry to admit that this is a signpost to pride that has popped up in my own life many times. It appeared when that book *Praying for the World's 365 Most Influential People* was released. I have already noted that when I received my copy, I fell into the sin of pride, and the way I did this was by keeping score.

My pride did not lie in appearing in the same book with the likes of Saddam Hussein, the Dali Lama or Ted Turner. Nor did I have any feelings of superiority over other Christian leaders who were featured in the book. In fact, just the opposite occurred: I wondered how I even got in there with them. But then I started making mental lists of Christian leaders who were *not* in the book. I found myself especially enjoying the fact that my most outspoken critics were not listed! What I had begun doing *was* keeping score. Pride and superiority were making me feel good!

Three Weeks of Spiritual Ups and Downs

Through the conviction of the Holy Spirit, I quickly realized that I was sinning! Therefore, I did what I knew I was supposed to do: I confessed my sin and God forgave me as He said He would. But a day or two later I found myself having another good time by keeping score again. I must admit that it took three whole weeks of spiritual ups and downs before I finally gained a victory over that fleshly sin of pride. Happily, once I did gain victory, the pride never returned. Now I do not even have a copy of that book in my library. For me to have that book would be like a person with a sexual addiction having a copy of *Playboy*! I do not want anything to do with it!

In my opinion, keeping score does not apply to a healthy process of measuring progress toward a goal. If you are a real estate broker, for example, and you have a goal of doing $2 million worth of business in a particular year, you should measure your progress. If you have determined to reduce your golf score by four strokes, if you need to lose 35 pounds or if your basketball team strives to lead the league, naturally you count. I have a personal goal for writing books, for example. I set the goal because a number of years ago someone asked me how many books I intended to write in my life. I had not thought about that before, but I responded that I probably should have a biblical goal, so why not aim for 66 books—the number of books in the Bible? I am keeping close enough track to know that this book is number 61. I do not think that monitoring this kind of progress is pride, but the minute I begin comparing what I write to other authors, I would be keeping score. I do not want to do that!

SIGNPOST 3: CULTIVATING A CREATOR COMPLEX

We know that we have a "creator complex" when we begin to evaluate the lives and ministries of other people and compare them to who we are and what we do. To the degree that they do things differently, we tend to regard them as inferior. Then we try to change them and to make them over in our own image. It is OK to make people in your own image—if you are God. But if you are not God and you are trying to make others in your own image, then you may be playing God! That is a dangerous place to be.

Just like I am susceptible to keeping score, I have learned through the years that I am also very susceptible to the creator complex. In fact, in the year or so that I worked on this book, this signpost popped up a few times. I had to apologize to both individuals for unjustly demeaning them by expecting them to handle a situation just as I would have handled it.

One friend, for example, seemed to me to be taking too much time writing a book and not paying enough attention to an important assignment that I had contracted with him to do. I was irritated, and I made the mistake of informing him that it did not take me nearly as long to write a book. He looked back at me and replied, "How can you expect me to write books like you?" Fortunately, I immediately recognized the creator-complex signpost and I apologized on the spot. I then confessed it as a sin of pride, and God forgave me. But I know that I continue to be vulnerable in this area and that I have to keep my guard up at all times.

The Fine Line

I have found that there is a very fine line between fulfilling my responsibility as a leader, a teacher, a mentor and a role model on the one hand and succumbing to a creator complex on the other. Part of me wants to be like the apostle Paul and authentically say "Imitate me" (1 Cor. 4:16) to those under my spiritual leadership. When it comes right down to it, if I cannot say that, I cannot really be the leader or the role model that I am supposed to be. I cannot keep my integrity and, at the same time, suggest to those who follow me: "Do as I say, don't do as I do!" Having people follow my example is one part of me—another part wants to avoid the creator complex.

I am discovering that this becomes especially sensitive when writing a book on humility. I can hardly write a book such as this without, from time to time, giving my personal opinion on behavior traits that I have decided either to adopt or to avoid. Some readers will undoubtedly disagree with some of my points. I can hear them saying, with certain irritation, "Peter is plagued by the very creator complex he is trying to warn us against. He is trying to make me over in his image!" So it is not easy to write a book such as this and at the same time totally avoid giving others the idea that they need to use me as a measurement scale.

The basic issue is that a role model is just that—a personal example for others to follow if they choose to do so. That is what "imitate me" means. But the creator complex kicks in when we go on from there and begin to evaluate the worth and dignity of an individual by how closely they match our own examples. This turns a suggestion or an admonition into coercion and manipulation, and the line has been crossed to the creator complex.

SIGNPOST 4: REJOICING IN OTHERS' FAILURES AND RESENTING OTHERS' SUCCESSES

The wording of this common signpost of pride practically says it all. Who has not experienced the temptation of rejoicing in others' failures and resenting others' successes?

The soil that nourishes this root of pride is carnal competition. Having noted this, let's admit that there are certainly many areas of normal life where competition is healthy, meaning that competition *in and of itself* is not necessarily bad. I strongly believe in the merits of a free enterprise society, for example, and free enterprise is based on the assumption that competition tends to increase the quantity and the quality of goods and services. I, for one, am glad that United Parcel Service and FedEx are giving the United States Postal Service competition in expediting the delivery of packages and letters. By contrast, communism failed as a socioeconomic design largely because it prohibited competition.

However, among Christian leaders, personal competition is wrong. This is where competition can become carnal. The biblical teaching that the eye cannot say to the hand "I have no need of you" (1 Cor. 12:21) is a blanket prohibition of competition. If Christian leaders are playing tennis or golf with each other, competition in that arena is acceptable and even expected. But the idea of one ministry or church growing at the expense of another is a wide-open door to pride on the part of the leaders involved.

Are there any pastors who feel good when another church in town undergoes a disagreeable split? Are there ministry leaders who secretly enjoy the news that a similar ministry is having financial problems and cannot meet payroll? Unfortunately, you and I both know that it is not unusual for pastors and ministry leaders to harbor such feelings. The reason for this is an ungodly sense of competition accompanied by the idea that your loss is my gain.

Do you find yourself getting irritated when someone else receives a tremendous blessing? If you do, take it as someone waving signpost 4 in front of you and turn around. Renew your mind. Never allow your mind to despise another person's gain. Rejoice when a friend gets a newer and larger car, when they are invited to appear on an influential TV show, when the attendance at their conference is greater than the attendance at yours and when they lose weight, but you cannot seem to do it!

Richard J. Foster takes this point one step further suggesting that when you find yourself in a competitive situation you should actually pray that the other person will be more outstanding, more praised and more used of God. Foster writes, "Pull for them and rejoice in their successes. . . . If you will do this faithfully . . . you will really and truly be learning to 'Do nothing from selfish ambition or conceit, but with humility [regard] others as better than yourselves' (Phil. 2:3, *RSV*)."[5]

Part of humility is a willingness to be underestimated or slighted and to feel no resentment.

Here is how Andrew Murray put it: "The humble man feels no jealousy or envy. He can praise God when others are preferred and blessed before him. He can bear to hear others praised and himself forgotten, because in God's presence he has learned to say with Paul, "I am nothing" (2 Cor. 12:11).[6] Part of humility is a willingness to be underestimated or slighted and to feel no resentment.

SIGNPOST 5: COMPULSIVELY DEFENDING YOURSELF AGAINST CRITICISM

One obvious signpost along the road to pride has to do with the way we react to criticism. By definition, criticism is emotionally distressing. The natural response to criticism is to fight back. When critics say that we are wrong, we then feel obligated to prove that we are right.

When we do this, we attempt to make ourselves look good by proving that our accusers are wrong. When we take that approach, even if we succeed, there are no winners. We both lose. We lose because we have succumbed to pride.

It is much better to let the critics have their say. For a starter, we should leave an opening in our minds for the possibility that they may be right. This may take time. When we first hear the criticism, we may be too upset to absorb it. But we should always process it over time before deciding whether the criticism is justified or not. If it is, we should not hesitate to admit it and thank our critic for helping us think better. If the criticism is, in fact, unjustified, why not take the high road? Why not just move on with life and pray that God will bless the critic?

I like Murray's advice on this matter. He writes, "Let us look on every brother or sister who tries or vexes us as God's means of grace. Let us look on him or her as God's instrument for our purification."[7]

IF YOU TURN AROUND, YOU WILL BE BETTER OFF!

Whenever you see one of these signposts marking the road to pride, turn around and go the other way. You will be better off for it. And please do not wait until it is too late!

JOURNAL QUESTIONS

1. Write a definition of "pride." How is pride different from self-esteem?

2. When it comes to pride, are you on a bad road or a good road? Which of the five signposts of pride can you find in your life? How have these signposts and pride manifested themselves? Do you yearn for praise? Keep score? Cultivate a creator complex?

3. Think of a time when a colleague or competitor of yours has failed. What was your response? Now, think of a time when a colleague or competitor has succeeded. What was your response?

4. Make a list of criticisms people have raised about you and note what your response was to each critical comment. How did your response fare when measured against the goal of humility?

JOURNAL NOTES

A man's pride will bring him low, but the
humble in spirit will retain honor.

PROVERBS 29:23

_____

_____

_____

_____

_____

_____

_____

_____

_____

IF MY PEOPLE, WHO ARE CALLED
BY MY NAME, WILL HUMBLE
THEMSELVES AND PRAY AND SEEK
MY FACE AND TURN FROM THEIR
WICKED WAYS, THEN WILL I HEAR
FROM HEAVEN AND WILL
FORGIVE THEIR SIN AND WILL
HEAL THEIR LAND.

2 Chronicles 7:14, *NIV*

Ten Signposts Along the Road to Humility

Once you decide to turn away from the five signposts on the road to pride and to keep clear of the false humility attached to legalism, then you are ready to move down the wonderful road toward God-pleasing humility. This is the way that you humble yourself. You begin to follow these 10 signposts on your life journey. If you do this sincerely, God will be the One who sees to it that you are ultimately exalted.

SIGNPOST 1: CAREFULLY ADHERING TO THE BIBLICAL RULES FOR SUBMISSION

It is a sad fact that in today's society, submission has almost become a countercultural notion. It is sad because this modern mind-set obstructs our ability to be the kind of biblical believers that we are supposed to be. The Bible teaches that every one of us has a duty to be submissive. I have already quoted 1 Peter 5:5, which clearly presents the idea that we all need to clothe ourselves with humility. The same verse also declares: "Yes, *all* of you be submissive to one another, and be clothed with humility, for God resists the proud, but gives grace to the humble" (emphasis added). I italicized the word "all" to help us keep in mind that each one of us must submit, not, of course, to every single person who touches our lives, but to certain people whom God has appropriately designated. Without biblical submission, no one can be truly humble.

What, then, is God's design for submission?

The Bible is quite specific about this. A glance at the words "submit" and "submission" found in most concordances reveals many principles of submission. Here are a few of the better-known examples:

- **Citizens must submit to their government.** "Therefore *submit* yourselves to every ordinance of man for the Lord's sake, whether to the king as supreme, or to governors, as to those who are sent by him for the punishment of evildoers and for the praise of those who do good" (1 Pet. 2:13-14, emphasis added).
- **Employees must submit to their supervisors.** "Servants, be *submissive* to your masters with all fear, not only to the good and gentle, but also to the harsh" (1 Pet. 2:18, emphasis added).

- **Wives must submit to their husbands.** "Wives, likewise, be *submissive* to your own husbands, that even if some do not obey the word, they, without a word, may be won by the conduct of their wives" (1 Pet. 3:1, emphasis added).
- **Young people must submit to older people.** "Likewise you younger people, *submit* yourselves to your elders" (1 Pet. 5:5, emphasis added).
- **Believers must submit to their pastors.** "Obey those who rule over you, and be *submissive*, for they watch out for your souls, as those who must give account" (Heb. 13:17, emphasis added).

These are just five biblical applications of submission. There are many more. Each one shows that humble people will willingly submit to those whom God has put in authority over them in every arena of life. Knowing when to submit and doing so should become an automatic component of our lifestyles. I think, for example, of the great apostle Paul on the island of Malta. People around him were cold and wet. So what did Paul do? He went out and gathered wood (see Acts 28:1-3). This was the kind of behavior that allowed God to exalt him.

SIGNPOST 2: UNDERSTANDING THE ROLE OF THE HOLY SPIRIT IN YOUR DAILY LIFE

I am aware that I have noted being filled with the Holy Spirit quite often. I do not mean to be redundant, but I am strongly convinced that personal touch with the activity of the Holy Spirit in our lives is absolutely essential for any one of us to achieve the true humility that God desires. Being filled with the Holy Spirit should not simply be an occasional experience, such as when you respond to an invitation to go up to the front of the church and find yourself lying on the floor for a period of time. This is good, and I recommend it; but being filled with the Holy Spirit should not only be an event—it should be a continuous condition.

Let me reiterate what I wrote earlier about being filled with the Holy Spirit. I noted that my preconversion lifestyle helped me to understand the Scripture "And do not be drunk with wine, in which is dissipation; but be filled with the Spirit" (Eph. 5:18).

> When your life is characterized by love, joy, peace, longsuffering, meekness (humility), self-control or the like, it is a result of the Holy Spirit operating in you.

Getting drunk lasts only one day. The writers of the Bible chose to use this as an analogy for being filled with the Holy Spirit. I believe that we are supposed to seek a new filling of the Holy Spirit every day.

How does this relate to humility?

Suppose you happen to do some really good things today. Why are you doing them? If you are filled with the Holy Spirit, you say "Thank You, Lord." In other words, you are not attributing certain accomplishments to some inherent superior quality that you have. Instead, you are acknowledging that the Holy Spirit has motivated and empowered you to do them.

That is the meaning of the fruit of the Spirit. When your life is characterized by love, joy, peace, longsuffering, meekness (humility), self-control or the like, it is a result of the Holy Spirit operating in you. God gets the credit, not you. If you practice thinking like this on a regular basis, you will be well on your way to humility.

SIGNPOST 3: DISCOVERING YOUR SPIRITUAL GIFTS

During the time I was writing this book, I read a research report by George Barna. I was appalled by his conclusion that the level of practical knowledge about spiritual gifts has dropped dramatically among believers across the board during a five-year period around the turn of the millennium. This is a startling piece of information because it has the potential of affecting the body of Christ profoundly in the days to come. It obviously threatens to handicap Christian ministry in local churches and to weaken the whole Christian movement. While this danger merits considerable attention, in this chapter I simply want to focus on how an incomplete understanding of spiritual gifts can affect humility.

True Destiny

Let me once again note Romans 12:3. This is where the Bible instructs us to think soberly of ourselves as God has dealt to each one a measure of faith. What is this measure of faith? The following verses go on to point out that we are all members of the body of Christ and that we all have our own God-given spiritual gifts. In other words, once you discover your spiritual gifts, you will then have the right mind-set to understand who God has made you to be. It puts you in realistic touch with your true destiny.

If you are at all analytical about your behavior, you will realize that you do certain things much better than you do other things. I am not referring to the character issues that I mentioned in reference to the last signpost. I am referring to tasks. When certain tasks that you do well are a recognized aspect of Christian ministry, you then should realize that it is not really you who are doing them on your own; it is God working in you through the gifts He has given you. You may be better than average at teaching, administration, hospitality, prophecy or intercession. You have no grounds to be proud of these gifts because you did not generate them through your own ability or goodness. God, for His own reasons, chose to give them to you. Yes, you can be thankful for them and excited about using them, but you cannot be *proud* of them.

Here is what can happen if you do not understand what your spiritual gifts are and how they operate.

Your Strengths

Suppose that there is some task, related to ministry, that you do well. For example, I write books well. By this I do not mean that I am the best writer in the world. I know for a fact that I am not because none of my books has ever been on any best-seller list. But I also know that, at least, I write better than the average person. There are two ways that I could explain to others how I came about this ability to write books.

The first explanation could be one that many Christians decide to use because, ironically, it is intended as an expression of humility. Instead it turns out to be a form of phony or even reverse humility. I could say, "Oh, itty-bitty me? I'm nothing! I'm a worm! I'm no better than anyone else! I'm just a mere human being! If I can write books, anyone can write books! Writing books is nothing—you could write books just as easily as I can!"

Consider what this does to other people. It unintentionally plants a negative self-image in their minds. Why? Because they are realistic. They know full well that they belong to the great majority of people in the human race who will never write a book. However, when I say "itty-bitty me," what I am telling them is that if they just *wanted* to write a book enough they could do it. They then conclude that I must *want* to write more than they do. Therefore I must be more diligent, more disciplined, more energetic, more hardworking, more motivated, more persistent, more in touch with what God is saying and more accomplished than they are. This is why such a concept turns out to be *reverse* humility. Ironically, instead of appearing more humble, I end up appearing superior. This turns out to be a sneaky way to exalt myself!

God's Choice!

Let's look at another possible explanation. I could just as well say, "The reason that I write books well is because God has chosen to give me a spiritual gift of teaching that He has guided me to exercise through the printed page. This is *charisma*, a grace-gift that I in no way ever deserved. It was God's choice, but once He decided to give me the gift, I gratefully accepted it. My ability to write comes through the work of the Holy Spirit in me, not through my natural abilities or any superior quality that I might have of being able to work harder and longer than others."

God has likewise given spiritual gifts to every member of the body of Christ so that the Church functions as it should through the ministry of all the saints. Other saints might not write as well as I do, but they might evangelize better, be more hospitable, prophesy more accurately, care more compassionately for others, preach more powerfully, cast out more demons or serve as better administrators. How do they do this? Because God has chosen to give them spiritual gifts that He has not given me, and the Body of Christ needs them just as much or more than it needs my books!

This second approach has not injured anyone. Rather, it has helped and empowered people to be what God wants them to be, instead of subtly suggesting that they try hard to be more like me. It has also enabled me to be humble, instead of exalting myself!

Insecurity and Pride

Let me add one more brief note on the value of discovering your spiritual gifts. Once you know your gifts and are comfortable ministering in those gifts, you gain a tremendous sense of fulfillment in ministry. In other words, it builds a healthy personal security and self-esteem. This is important because, psychologically speaking, there is a direct discernable relationship between pride and personal insecurity. Insecure people tend to compensate through expressions of pride. You can avoid this trap by realistically coming to terms with your spiritual gifts.

SIGNPOST 4: KNOWING YOUR PLACE IN THE BODY

This signpost is closely tied with the previous one. The most common biblical analogy for understanding how spiritual gifts operate is with the human body. This makes it simple, because we all know enough about our human bodies to agree that a heart is clearly different from a liver but that they need each other. Our eyes need our brain. Within our eye, our retina needs our eyelid.

This analogy applies directly to ministry within the Body of Christ. If you are following signpost 3, then you understand what your spiritual gifts are and how you personally minister in them. Now go one step further. It really is just as important to know what spiritual gifts you *don't* have as it is to know what spiritual gifts you *do* have! In other words, it would be ridiculous if my big toe tried to do the work of my ear or if my tongue tried to do the work of my nose.

A Prophetic Disaster!

I have messed up in the area of knowing my place in the Body more than once. For example, I will never forget one major Global

Harvest Ministries conference. It was a huge gathering and incredible spiritual power was being released. Among other things, a lot of prophecy was going on from the platform. If anyone had asked me before the conference, I would have told them that I do not have the gift of prophecy—in my half century of being a Christian, I have never thought that I had it and no one else has ever confused me with a prophet! But during the conference a friend whom I greatly respect suggested that in order to validate my apostolic role, I had better get up and prove to the people that I could prophesy. The excitement and emotion of the moment exceeded any better judgment I might have had, so I went up on the platform and started prophesying. It was a disaster! I knew in my mind before I was halfway through that what was coming forth were just human, unanointed words! I cut it as short as I could and sat down, inwardly embarrassed.

When it came right down to it, I ended up as a toe trying to be an ear! I know that I have the gift of an apostle, but I also know that I cannot be the apostle that God wants me to be without constantly receiving the ministry of prophets. I must be humble enough to admit that I cannot do it all and that I am incomplete without others. When I started acting like a prophet, I was exalting myself—and I learned my lesson.

The Acknowledgment of Others

Realizing that you need others applies not only to recognizing those who have other spiritual gifts, but it can also apply to your relationships with those who have the same gift. If you are humble, you will not deny the gifts and the work of the Holy Spirit in your own ministry. However, you will also acknowledge that you are not the only one to whom God has given that gift and that many others might have an even higher and more effective measure of it. You will not attempt to compensate for your own limitations by subtly putting down others who may actually be better than yourself.

A Good Example

I remember once when Mike Bickle, leader of the International House of Prayer in Kansas City, was speaking at one of our conferences. He was on a roll—both he and the audience were having a wonderful time. At one point he paused and said words to this effect: "I'm giving you this teaching, and I think it's pretty good. [It was!] But [he pointed his finger and gave a wry smile to let us know that he was joking] my angel is standing right over there, looking at me and saying, 'You don't know anything!' He is right! I only know about 1 percent of this subject! Many others know much more!" Then he went on with his incredible message.

When I heard him, I said to myself, *Mike Bickle has really learned how to humble himself! I want to be like that!*

SIGNPOST 5: KNOWING THE DIFFERENCE BETWEEN YOUR STRENGTHS AND WEAKNESSES

I like what John Stott says: "Humility is not another word for hypocrisy; it is another word for honesty. Humility is not pretending to be other than what we are, but acknowledging the truth about what we are."[1]

We need to get rid of the notion that as soon as we recognize and verbalize to others that we have certain strengths, we have somehow fallen into pride. This is especially true once we are filled with the Holy Spirit and we are ministering in the spiritual gifts that God has given to us. The eye would not deny the fact that it can see or the stomach that it can digest or the leg that it can jump, even if no other member of the body can do what it does. It is not pride, because that member of the body is simply doing what it was designed to do.

One of the things that God designed me to do, for example, is to teach. I have the gift of teaching because God Himself made that choice for me. It is, therefore, one of my strengths. From time to time someone who has heard me will come up to me later and say, "Peter, you're such a good teacher!" It would not only be stupid for me to deny that, but it would also be ungrateful to God. I am a good teacher, thanks only to the ongoing work of the Holy Spirit in me. I certainly can be, and I hope to be, a better teacher someday than I am now, but that is not the point. My response to the person who tells me that I am a good teacher is "Thank you." And depending upon the context and what is appropriate for the moment, I may well add "And I thank God for the gift He has given me."

By asserting this, I am certainly not trying to leave the impression that I am the best. In fact, I fully realize that I am not the best teacher in the world. In fact for years I have been reminded of this twice a month when I listen to tapes by John Maxwell, my personal paragon of a teacher. I still say to myself, *When I grow up, I want to teach like John Maxwell teaches!*

Facing Weaknesses

On the other hand, I had better not deny my weaknesses. Probably because I am a cofounder of the World Prayer Center in Colorado Springs, recognized as an apostle of the global prayer movement, and author of the *Prayer Warrior* series, people from time to time will come up to me and say, "Peter, you're such a powerful prayer warrior!" When that happens, my response is very simple: "No, I'm not!"

I do associate professionally and on an ongoing basis with a significant number of world-class prophetic intercessors. If anyone knows what powerful prayer warriors are, I do. As a result, I have no question in my mind that I am not one of them. In fact, I am so poor at the kind of strategic praying they do that it is almost embarrassing. When I do pray with them, I understand what it might be like for a high school baseball player to be hanging around the Los Angeles Dodgers' training camp. I will confess that I have a deep desire in my heart to pray in public like my pastor, Ted Haggard, does. But even though I have listened to him for years and have tried to imitate him as much as I can, I have never even come close. That is one reason that I try to pray in public as little as possible.

Knowing What You Don't Know

If you are humble, you will readily admit that there are many things you do not know. This is a hard thing for some. You will rarely, if ever, hear certain people answer a question with "I don't know!" Prideful people seem to develop a mechanism to prevent them from ever being impressed with what someone else tells them. No one can ever seem to give them information that they have not already heard. They have a way of faking or exaggerating knowledge, especially if the topic is related to a field in which they are expected to have a degree of expertise.

> If you are humble, you will readily admit that there are many things you do not know.

One-upmanship is a major manifestation of pride. Whenever someone shares what he has done or seen, the prideful person has done or seen something bigger and will surely talk about it. The prideful person cannot stand to come in second—he has to be number one. He may not even realize that every time he does this, he is belittling the other person. This is not the way to go. Instead, you must be very free to admit our weaknesses, lack of knowledge, inexperience and shortcomings. You should always make others feel that they are teaching you new things, and you need to get excited about it. When you learn to do this, you will be on the road to humility.

SIGNPOST 6: DARING TO BE REALISTIC ABOUT YOUR SUCCESSES AND FAILURES

Some Christians live what appears to be extremely dull lives. They do not have many exhilarating victories, nor do they have many devastating defeats. They seem to live in a la-la land where everything that happens is just about what is supposed to happen—so what does it all matter anyway? On the one hand, they may imagine that if they claim resounding success at any task, it would certainly be seen as pride. On the other hand, they may fear that if they admit that they truly bombed on some other task, it would be questioning the power of God. I believe that both of these extremes should be avoided.

The election of George W. Bush as president of the United States quite naturally received vast media coverage. One interesting thing about the election was that the winner happened to be the son of a former president, George Bush. I recall that in one interview, the elder Bush said words to the effect, "I hope people understand that they are looking at the proudest father in the U.S.A.!" This kind of pride should not be interpreted as lack of humility. Satisfaction in raising a child who becomes president of the United States in all probability will not provoke the resistance of God as other forms of more carnal pride tend to do. In fact, Paul himself made a point of *boasting* about his children in the faith in Corinth (see 2 Cor. 7:4).

I started my school, Wagner Leadership Institute, in 1998, with the first classes in 1999. My goal was to have 150 students by the end of 1999. I must say that I had a great deal of personal satisfaction in being able to announce that we had more than 150 students at the end of the first year. I personally did not feel that this was a manifestation of what Andrew Murray would call "devilish pride." I had prayed for this, and I gave God the glory. But still, it did not inhibit me from rejoicing in the accomplishment.

Discouraging Failures

By contrast, I have seen more than a few discouraging failures in my life. However, I have never been reluctant to admit it when I have failed. For example, I earned varsity letters in baseball during my last three years of high school. While playing baseball, there were times when I came up to bat with runners in scoring position and the game on the line. There was no question in my mind that if I struck out, I had failed—f-a-i-l-e-d! Even though I always lost sleep over it that night, I would not try to rationalize it. Refusing to admit that failure is failure, especially when we blame that failure on someone else, is no way to nurture humility.

On a more specific note, a large portion of my ministry career has been spent in teaching the principles of church growth. One of my notable failures was undertaking to edit an encyclopedia of church growth. I invested a lot of energy in that project, and I found that I simply could not accomplish it. Whatever it took to produce such an encyclopedia, I did not have it. Later, my friend and student, Elmer Towns, picked up the project and the encyclopedia has now been published—and it included only a few of my articles. Elmer clearly has something that I do not, and I am proud of him, just as a teacher should be!

A major principle of church growth has been, is and will continue to be what is called the homogeneous unit principle.[2] Even though it is a valid sociological and missiological principle, the strenuous efforts that I have made to communicate it over decades to the general public, for all intents and purposes, have failed. I have even been accused of racism because of my efforts! This has been one of my major life disappointments.[3]

At the same time, another task of mine was to contextualize or adapt the teachings of Donald McGavran's Church Growth Movement to the American scene. McGavran had done all of his research on Church growth in India and other Third World nations. After he invited me to join him on the faculty of the Fuller Seminary School of World Mission, I set out to research and write on how McGavran's principles might apply to American churches. In this endeavor my 20 years of effort turned out to be successful. Not long ago, I was unashamed to spend some moments in personal satisfaction when a scholarly article documenting the fact that I had achieved my goal was published in the *Journal of the American Society for Church Growth*.[4] An inexorable principle of life is that you win some and you lose some!

SIGNPOST 7: TAKING RISKS

Deep within the nature of a risk is the possibility of failure. This is, unfortunately, more than some people can handle. But humble people are willing to take risks, because they are willing to lose. Not that they want to lose or plan to lose; they naturally want to win. But they also know that there is a crucial difference between losing and being a loser.

This became clear to me as I watched the ministry of David Yonggi Cho of Korea, for years the pastor of the largest church in the world, the Yoido Full Gospel Church. As a member of Cho's international board, I enthusiastically joined him in the goal that he set for the evangelization of Japan. Toward the beginning of the 1990s, Cho was visiting Japan once a month and projecting a goal of 10 million born-again Japanese believers by the year 2000. This was a substantial risk, since, of all of the nations of the world, Japan has notoriously been one of the most resistant to the gospel. I went on record as believing, with Cho, that the goal would be reached, and I thought that I had some substantial missiological data on which to base my hopes.

However, the year 2000 came and went without the goal being reached. In fact, it was not even close. During the decade of the 1990s the rate of church growth in Japan remained virtually unchanged, and 2000 saw fewer than 1 million born-again believers there—obviously far short of the goal of 10 million.

Few would deny that Cho, as a Christian leader, has been exalted. He is widely acknowledged as one of the most influential individuals of our time. Why did God choose to exalt him? He obviously would have passed the tests of humility back in his formative years. The Japan incident helped verify this. Before the year 2000 ended, Cho, now in his mature years, admitted publicly in his newsletter that he realized he had set the goal of 10 million believers in his own flesh, not through a direct and verifiable word from God. Only a truly humble leader would make such an admission.

Controversial Enterprises

Many leaders face the choice as to whether or not they should launch some risky enterprise that has the potential of becoming controversial. Because they are humble, they refuse to be daunted by questions such as:

- *What will people say?*
- *Will I be considered unbalanced?*
- *Does this jeopardize my career?*

They are willing to take such risks because they know that preserving the status quo is not necessarily a badge of humility.

At this writing, one of my assignments from God is to lead the International Coalition of Apostles as the presiding apostle. Because this is such a new enterprise, I could not do it without taking substantial risks. A major risk involves my responsibility to make sure that all ICA members are legitimate apostles. This is clearly a risk because, at least in the early stages of our existence as a group, we have no widespread consensus as to the exact qualifications of a legitimate apostle. I have my own ideas, but if I turn out to be mistaken, I am willing to be wrong and admit it. Will I make mistakes? I have no question that I will. Some will undoubtedly become members whom I should not have approved. But I believe that the net result will be positive and the risks will have been worth taking.

What other option do I have? To wait until our definition of apostle is perfect and then progress in a fail-safe mode? My fear is that if I chose that approach, God's *kairos* moment (proper time) might pass us by forever. In my mind we would be worse off in that scenario than we would in taking the risk now.

One of John Maxwell's most popular books is *Failing Forward*. I love that book because it puts a positive spin on taking risks, whether you win some or lose some. Not being afraid to fail, even when there is the possibly that you would look bad if you fall short, is a sure mark of humility!

SIGNPOST 8: ACCEPTING PRAISE BUT REJECTING FLATTERY

If you truly accomplish something significant in life and are praised for it, you should receive the praise with dignity. Refusing to accept legitimate praise is not a sign of humility; it is a sign of insecurity.

Andrew Murray saw through this potential façade of low self-esteem. Here is the way he expressed it: "I fear that there are many who have sought to humble themselves by strong expressions of self-condemnation and self-denunciation."[5] This ironically turns out to be an approach toward proving to others that you are superspiritual. Murray affirms that such a carnal approach usually does not work out well. He astutely observes that many such people "yet have to confess with sorrow that a humble spirit, accompanied by kindness, compassion, meekness, and forbearance, is still as far off as ever."[6]

A Fine Line

It may be a fine line, but it is helpful to be aware that there is a difference between well-deserved praise and self-serving, insincere flattery. Some people may try to gain favor with you by flattery, and humble people will politely reject that.

For example, at the writing of this book I have arrived at that stage in life at which my friends and I tend to talk about our age, rather than keep it a secret, which we might have done in years past. I therefore frequently mention that I am 71. But from time to time someone who hears this will say, "Peter, you don't look 71!" Such a statement has clearly crossed the line into flattery. The fact of the matter is that I *am* 71 and because of that, I necessarily *look* 71. When I hear that, my response is, "Yes, I do. I look 71 because I am 71!" The exchange usually draws a nervous laugh, and because it is a trivial matter, we quickly go on to a different subject.

Accepting flattery is closely akin to accumulating solicited praise. I recently saw a book written by a well-known author and published by a well-known Christian publisher with 26 paragraph-long expressions of solicited praise for the author and the book—all 26 appeared in the front of the book before the title page! This, in my opinion, far exceeds the normal industry standard of three or four endorsements, and it can be interpreted as projecting feelings of insecurity that humble people do not usually allow to surface.

SIGNPOST 9: AVOIDING LIVING IN THE ACHIEVEMENTS OF THE PAST

The present should be seen as a stepping-stone into the future, not a slippery slide to the past. Think about it: There is no future in living in the past.

This brings to mind my favorite radio program when I was in elementary school, "The Lone Ranger." This was in the 1930s, before the advent of television. In each program something dramatic would occur: A rancher was losing cattle to rustlers, stagecoaches kept getting robbed, someone was being swindled out of a gold mine or a defenseless woman was in distress. At the climax of each program, the crisis seemed hopeless and the bad guys seemed to be headed toward victory. Then, out of nowhere, the Lone Ranger came on the scene, he fired a few silver bullets, and suddenly everything was all right—the good guys lived happily ever after. The part I liked best was at the end when the astounded rancher or the breathless woman or the dumbfounded stagecoach driver, reveling in their unexpected good fortune, would exclaim, "Who was that masked man?" There was never any answer except, heard in the distance, "Hi-yo Silver! Away!"

No one could have written a biography of the Lone Ranger—nobody even knew his name! The Lone Ranger taught me way back then that it was not too important who knew your name or who associated it with accomplishments of the past, no matter how heroic. After the successful event, the most important thing was to focus on helping the next rancher or woman who might be in trouble.

Christian Biographies

My close friends and my publisher have known for a long time that I will not allow a biography to be written on my life. I personally cannot get interested in reading Christian biographies because of their propensity toward living in the achievements of the past. However, I must admit that this may be a personal idiosyncrasy and not a general principle of humility. For example, John Stott, whom I earlier cited as an outstanding contemporary role model for humility, has authorized Timothy Dudley-Smith to write his biography.

Whatever your view on Christian biographies, we can all heed the principle that it is good to learn lessons from the past but not to revel in the victories of the past. Do not make a personal highlight film and keep replaying it!

SIGNPOST 10: HAVING THE ABILITY TO PASS ON YOUR GLORY TO OTHERS

The Bible declares, "Let nothing be done through selfish ambition or conceit, but in lowliness of mind let each esteem others better than himself" (Phil. 2:3). This is one of the most radical statements on humility ever written. In fact it is the lead-in to the famous passage on Christ's humility in agreeing to leave heaven to come to Earth and to live, for a time, as a human being. We are instructed to "let this mind be in you which was also in Christ" (Phil 2:5).

Esteeming others better than yourself is not easy, even if you decide that you want to do it. It is an essential step, however, if you are on the road to humility and if you want to arrive. On the one hand, you must take credit when credit is due. On the other hand, you must give credit when credit is due. If you err, it is better to err on the side of giving too much credit to others, as long as it is not phony.

Never resent others getting public acclaim for something in which you might have had a part, sometimes a major part, in making happen. If you feel you have been slighted, keep your feelings to yourself. If you have an idea which someone else takes and gets credit for, the best thing for you to do is to get another idea, not to claim the honor for yourself. When you are bypassed, even unjustly, never be defensive.

Stolen Words

I learned this back in the 1970s when I was younger and having more battles with pride than I do now. A friend of mine enrolled in one of my courses. Some months later, he published a book that contained not only my thoughts but also my word-for-word outline. I was incensed! He had robbed me! I sat down and wrote him a torrid letter of condemnation, ripping him apart for his flagrant disregard for basic Christian ethics and his violation of my intellectual and literary rights!

In those days I was teaching at Fuller Seminary and my wife, Doris, was my administrative assistant. I gave her the handwritten draft to type, which she did. But when she finished, she brought the letter into my office and said with no hesitation, "You aren't going to send this letter!" Needless to say, I never sent it! It went into the file and it has long since been purged.

The upshot? My friend and I are still friends! I do not think he has any idea that I ever even knew that he used my outline in his book. Thanks to Doris, we all came out winners, and I learned my lesson. I have never done anything like that since, even though I cannot count the number of times I have seen similar things happen to me across the years. But my attitude is now entirely different. I look at myself as an idea broker, and I now *rejoice* when I see my ideas getting fed back to me, with or without proper credit! In fact I now routinely refer to the copyright line on my lesson notes, explaining to my students that it means "When you copy the notes, copy them right!"

Compulsive Interrupting

Compulsive interrupting can be a sneaky manifestation of pride, especially for people who have quick minds. Something another person says may trigger a thought. Instead of patiently waiting to see if an opportunity might come up to express that thought, a prideful person will act on impulse and cut the other person off, because he or she is convinced that the thought simply cannot wait. When you do that, you are subtly telling the other person that your thought is *more important* right now than anything they have to say. Humble people do not do that. They esteem others more highly than themselves.

The road to humility? Yes, you can take the trip and arrive!

JOURNAL QUESTIONS

1. How is submission related to humility?

2. What are your spiritual gifts? How will knowing and operating in these gifts help you advance along the road to humility?

3. How does taking risks result in humility? What risks have you taken in your life, and what have been the results?

4. Make a list of your past achievements. Now throw away that piece of paper. How will not living in the past create more humility in your life? How can you pass on the glory for success to others?

JOURNAL NOTES

Let nothing be done through selfish ambition or conceit,
but in lowliness of mind let each esteem others
better than himself.

PHILIPPIANS 2:3

_____

_____

_____

_____

_____

_____

_____

_____

_____

_____

_____

_____

_____

_____

WHEN THEY CAST YOU DOWN,
AND YOU SAY, "EXALTATION WILL
COME!" THEN HE WILL SAVE
THE HUMBLE PERSON.

Job 22:29

How Humility Helps Defuse Adversity

Humility, like other Christian virtues, has not been given to us by God as a chain around our necks to make life miserable. Just the opposite is true. If we live life as God deigns it to be lived, we will be the happiest people on Earth. Humility will boost us, not burden us.

A practical example of this is how humility can help defuse the adversity that inevitably comes our way. I am excited about this chapter because it will show just how beneficial humility can be in our daily lives.

For a good part of my life I have had to deal with adversity. I am not referring to falling off a ladder, the computer crashing after a day's work, suffering from diabetes, the car needing a new engine or the death of a family member. Those are bona fide adversities but of a different type. In this chapter, I am focusing on the kind of adversity that emerges from personal relationships. I want to concentrate on criticism from other people. I want to show how humility can help us deal with problems produced in our lives by those around us.

HISTORY MAKERS

Not everyone experiences the same degree of adversity that is brought on by others. It depends somewhat on how each of us relates to history. There are some people who love to read history; others analyze and teach history; some write about history, and others have learned to make good use of the lessons of history. But members of another group literally *make* history. I suspect that you want to be part of this latter group. You want to be a history maker. You want your life to make a difference.

If that is the case, I have a warning for you. Those who make history tend to run into more adversity in their lives than those who are content with the status quo.

Think for a moment about those individuals who have their names in Church history books. They were rarely regarded as "balanced" men or women by their contemporaries. Why? Because they dared to color outside the lines. Invariably, anyone who chooses this road is criticized. Consider John Wesley, William Carey, Martin Luther and Aimee Semple McPherson. Look at the apostle Paul and Jesus Himself. Each one of them suffered adversity from those around them because they kept pulling people out of their comfort zones.

My name will not likely get into a Church history book; nonetheless I have lived my life as a risk taker. Consequently, I have received large quantities of criticism. A friend once referred to me as a "lightning rod." If I allowed criticism to damage me emotionally, I would be a basket case by now. Instead, I have grown in discovering how to make humility a part of my lifestyle, and that helps me to develop a tough skin. That is why I want to recommend humility to you as a major self-defense against adversity.

Follow Jesus' example. The Bible tells us to identify with Christ in His *death* (see Phil. 3:10). What does this mean? Before Jesus died, "He was reviled, [but] did not revile in return" (1 Pet. 2:23). Jesus was humble, and we are told to "let this mind be in you which was also in Christ Jesus" (Phil. 2:5).

FOUR LIFESTYLE QUALITIES

Adversity will certainly come if your life is making a difference. But before it does, there are four personal resolutions you should make that will keep you from throwing gasoline on those fires of adversity. Build these four qualities into your lifestyle so that they will always be there when the need arises. I promise that life will be better if you do.

1. **Do not harden your heart.** Always keep a soft heart that is ready to forgive others. Jesus taught us to pray: "Forgive us our sins, just as we have forgiven those who have sinned against us" (Matt. 6:12, *NLT*). In fact, if we ever harden our hearts and refuse to forgive others for what they have done to us, we run the risk of not having our own sins forgiven (see Matt. 6:14-15).

2. **Watch the nuances of your language.** Not only do we need to watch *what* we say, but we also need to watch *how* we say it. Just a twist of a word, a tone of voice, a cynical phrase or even the silent treatment can further provoke those who are inclined to be our adversaries.

Every morning I pray specifically against the temptation of using a sharp tongue.

3. **Do not dredge up past failures.** The person you are dealing with may have made serious mistakes that you happen to know about. Do not yield to the temptation to make that person look bad and put that person on the defensive by dredging up dirt. Deal only with present issues. If God forgets about past sins, so should we.

4. **Never say "I told you so!"** I constantly have to keep my guard up against this one because I often see future implications related to a current action before others may see them. Actually, saying "I told you so!" boils down to a manifestation of pride. Humility says to let another praise you, and if nobody happens to think of doing that, just stand back and let someone else get credit, even though you may think you deserve it.

Think of these four qualities as a lifestyle bank account that is always in the black and that you can draw on in whatever quantity as frequently as you wish. They may not prevent adversity from coming, but they will definitely keep it from getting out of hand.

NINE WAYS TO TURN ADVERSITY INTO ADVANTAGE

Adversity does not have to be negative. In fact, adversity has the potential of ending up as an advantage in our lives. I have already explained how, if we have decided to follow Jesus' desire that we humble ourselves, we will then be on the road to being exalted. That means that God will work in us (remember the passive verb?), helping us to make the right choices every time that adversity comes around. There are nine key choices that are easy to make if we choose to be humble.

Adversity has the potential of ending up as an advantage in our lives.

At this point, I want to be clear that I am not referring to drawing close to God, using our spiritual gifts or living a holy life, even though every one of these will also help when adversity comes. Rather, these nine suggestions are matters of the mind—how we *think*. Use them and you will find that adversity can make you a winner.

1. Keep the Long-Range View

Always be sure that you know where you are aiming to come out of a given situation when it is all over. When adversity shows up, it is all too easy to allow it to dominate your life and make you think that dealing with an immediate problem is all that matters. No. Keep the details of adversity in their proper perspective: They are only a small part of the big picture. Think of a football team. The long-range view is to score enough touchdowns to win the game, but the process will inevitably involve many plays that will result in lost yardage. Losing on a given play is not losing the game!

It will be a great help if you decide to major on the majors and minor on the minors. Knowing the difference between the two is part of smart workmanship. Working *hard* is important but not as important as working *smart*. Rather than invest too much in the glitches of adversity that certainly will come your way, use the limited amount of time and energy that you have at your disposal to contribute toward your long-range goals.

2. Admit That Your Critics May Be Right

Do not assume. Critics are not necessarily your enemies, although at times they may turn out to be. In most cases your critics are neither all right or all wrong. Your best starting point is to assume that they have something positive to contribute that will improve your conclusions. Try to get past the surface details of the criticism and find out the deeper motivation of your critics. Knowing their hearts will help you understand many nuances of what they say, and the criticism may turn out to be not as bad as it first sounded.

If we are humble, we will always be ready to change our minds, even though it may not be easy. I remember when I was trying to come up with a name for what I now call the New Apostolic Reformation. My first choice was postdenominationalism. It had taken me two years to come up with that term, and I had accumulated many solid arguments to justify it. But adversity soon came my way. Several of my friends who were denominational executives began criticizing me severely. I was trying to ignore them until on one occasion, in a small gathering of leaders, none other than Jack Hayford actually got angry at me—he told me what a terrible choice I had made. I made the mistake of arguing with him in that meeting; but later, after thinking about it, I realized that he was right. I wrote him a letter of apology and began looking for another name.

That particular adversity became an advantage, because I now am much happier with "New Apostolic Reformation" than I ever would have been with "postdenominationalism." Thank you, critics!

3. Love the Bride

I write Bride with a capital letter because I want it to refer to the Church, the Bride of Christ. To the degree that we have the mind of Christ, we will love the true Church, in all of its different forms, just as Christ loves His whole Bride.

If we keep this perspective, we can move ourselves beyond numerous issues that may cause adversarial attitudes in those who feel that their form of Church represents the only legitimate Bride of Christ. I think of the several snake-handling services that I have attended. Although I would not want to join in, I still see those rather unusual churches as part of the Bride. I prefer adult baptism to infant baptism. I prefer prophecy and healing to cessationism. I prefer the openness of God to classical theism. I prefer Wesleyan holiness to Reformed sanctification. I prefer contemporary worship to traditional worship. I prefer apostolic leadership to congregational government. I could go on to list many personal preferences. But having noted all of this—so what? Those who have preferences that differ from mine are as much a part of the Bride as those who agree with me.

4. Carefully Choose Your Battles

There is no good, compelling reason for you to fight every battle that comes your way. In fact, you would do well to decide ahead of time not only to choose carefully which battles you will fight but also to keep the number of battles as low as possible. You will be a much happier person if you know when to fight and when to fold.

> Decide ahead of time not only to choose carefully which battles you will fight but also to keep the number of battles as low as possible.

Without a long-range view, I could easily get embroiled in details, including terminology. For example, I do not particularly like some commonly-used terms such as "water baptism," "fivefold ministry," "Spirit-filled" or "end-time" as adjectives, or "clergy" as compared to "laity." I could use considerable energy in defending my point of view on each one of these terms, but these are battles that I have chosen not to fight.

I am constantly faced with pressure to take a public stand on certain issues, but to tackle them all would be, at least to me, an unfruitful diversion. Such endeavors would keep me from fulfilling the assignments that God has given me in this season. For example, I have chosen not to formulate strong opinions on topics such as animal noises in the Toronto blessing, the politics of Israel, seeker-sensitive churches, details of the great tribulation, stem cell research or the National Council of Churches. By making these choices, I am not trivializing the importance of the issues or demeaning those who give time and energy to them. Neither am I necessarily agreeing with one point of view or another. I am just saying that I have other battles to fight.

The battles that I have chosen to fight would include things such as pragmatic church growth, issues of cessationism, demonization of Christians, strategic-level spiritual warfare, contemporary offices of apostle and prophet, idolatry, power ministries, women in leadership and others. Every one of these areas has made me a target of criticism and adversity, but I am willing to pay whatever price is necessary to persuade others that my conclusions on these matters are correct. I can handle these battles because I have previously eliminated many others.

5. Always Think the Best of Others

Long ago I decided that when people come to me with criticism of others, I will not follow that trail unless the accusation deals with sex or money. If I feel any kind of a responsible relationship with the person who has been accused of misbehavior relating to sex or money, I will deal with it immediately and privately. If it is something else, I will give the accused person the benefit of the doubt and move ahead with other things.

What about heresy? In my mind the nonnegotiables are issues attached to the authority of Scripture and the person and work of

Jesus Christ. Beyond that I have a large range of tolerance for divergent points of view. I like the way Ted Haggard diagrams this in three concentric circles. The inner circle contains "absolutes," the next circle contains "interpretations," and the outer circle contains "deductions."[1] If we agree on the absolutes, let's recognize that the interpretations and deductions of others have been formed by a combination of family, friends, church traditions, temperaments, schooling, life experiences, culture and numbers of other influences. So have ours! These are areas for thinking the best of others and humbly admitting that they may be right!

6. Pick Winners and Ride Out the Rough Spots

Part of the role that we have as Christians is to help guide others along their road of discipleship. This can be in the family, in the church, in small groups, in the workplace, in ministries, or wherever. There is a great satisfaction in being able to help someone else get to the place where he is everything that God wants him to be.

During the decades that I taught at Fuller Seminary, I frequently did this by inviting individuals to teach with me in my courses. Whenever I came across someone whom I sized up as a winner and who knew more than I did about an area related to what I was teaching, I felt I could best serve my students by bringing that person into class as a visiting teacher. I have enjoyed doing this so much that I have compiled a private Wagner's List of individuals who now enjoy high visibility in ministry. They undoubtedly would have arrived there without me, but my satisfaction lies in the fact that God allowed me to have at least a small piece of the action.

However, it was not always easy. That is why I suggest riding out the rough spots once you have made your choice. I think of the late John Wimber, leader of the Vineyard Movement as an example. When I first met John, he was a relatively unknown associate pastor of a Quaker church. But I immediately perceived that he was much more skilled than I was in diagnosing the growth problems of congregations and in helping them to move in more productive directions. So I invited John to teach with me in my doctor of ministry courses. John was inexperienced in this kind of teaching, and at first he did not do well. His course evaluations were so bad that the head of the program called me in and requested that I dismiss John. This, obviously, became a major rough spot for me. But because I was convinced that I had a winner, I kept inviting him. In two or three years, John's evaluations were coming in better than mine! I can even say that I was proud of him—using the word "proud" in the healthy way.

7. Plan on Winning Some and Losing Some

I have actually made this point in an earlier chapter, but it is important enough to repeat. Humble people can take failure in stride. Insecure people habitually rationalize their failure. But rationalizing failure actually compounds the problem; it does not solve anything even though it may produce a superficial moment of emotional relief. Know that you are going to fail from time to time, and when you do so, admit it and move on.

While I have several names of people whom I have helped become winners on what I call Wagner's List, I hasten to note that I have missed it on occasion. A number of people whom I had sized up for high leadership potential turned out not to have it. It took me longer to recognize this in some cases than in others. But once I did recognize it, I immediately cut my losses and dropped them. I admitted I had been wrong, and I began looking for more winners.

8. Obey the Lord

Obeying the Lord is such a universal Christian ideal that some might wonder why I would even include it in this list. The answer lies in the fact that sometimes the adversity becomes so strong that you could collapse under its weight if you were not totally convinced that what you were doing was a literal assignment from God. This is how Martin Luther must have felt when he was being interrogated at the Diet of Worms. The consequences of his history-making ideas could have amounted to anything, even losing his life. Practically the whole world was against him. Former friends had become mortal enemies. Yet Luther's words have resounded through the ages: "Here I stand; I can do no other!"

One of the clearest and, at the same time, most unexpected assignments that I have received from God came at the famous 1989 Lausanne II congress on evangelism in Manila. It was there that God commissioned me to take international leadership in the area of what we were calling at the time "territorial spirits." As a consequence I founded the Spiritual Warfare Network, we began calling this "strategic-level spiritual warfare," I built it into the AD 2000 United Prayer Track, I taught courses on it at Fuller Seminary, I wrote three books on it, and I was a chief spokesperson for this type of ministry during the decade of the 1990s.

Adversity? I have been the target of more severe and prolonged criticism on this subject than anything else I have attempted. Whole books have been written against me, to say nothing of articles and sermons. My good friend John Wimber disagreed with me so much that we actually had to part ways. Because of a book written in German that accused me of being a heretic, I lost a grant of $1.5 million that had been promised me for the World Prayer Center facility. This was one of those cases in which I could have collapsed under the pressure had it not been for my strong underlying conviction that I was obeying the Lord!

There was much adversity, but obeying the Lord, as it usually does, turned it into an advantage.

9. Activate Your Prayer Shield

Looking back, I would have to conclude that more than anything else on this list, my team of intercessors has made the greatest contribution toward turning adversity into advantage. It was around the middle of the 1980s that Doris and I came to the realization that we needed help. We knew that we had moved to a level of ministry where we could not move ahead any longer without a serious group of personal intercessors whom God had assigned to pray for us on a daily basis. Ominous reports were coming to us that Satan had placed us on a higher position on his hit list—and we took those reports seriously.

That is when we began building a team of I-1, I-2 and I-3 intercessors. Since I have described and analyzed how this works in my book *Prayer Shield*, I will not repeat that here. But let me conclude this chapter with just one story about how it fleshes out in practice.

SHOWDOWN AT THE O.K. CORRAL

Picking up from what I said about adversity arising from my leadership in the field of strategic-level spiritual warfare, this adversity had also taken root among the faculty of Fuller Seminary's School of Theology. Reports came that there was a movement to dismiss me from the seminary, which undoubtedly would have happened if I had not previously been awarded academic tenure. Still, overt attempts were made to harass me, intimidate me and force me to back away from my position. I was called before the faculty senate to endure the nearest thing possible to a heresy trial. Things had come to a point where any remaining attitude of humility that I had was quickly evaporating. I had loaded my guns, and I was about ready to play academic and legal hardball.

At that point, President David Hubbard, now with the Lord, called an extraordinary meeting. He invited the key players in this drama over to his home one evening for "pie and coffee." I saw it as the equivalent to the showdown at the O.K. Corral, and I sent a red alert to my I-1 and I-2 intercessors. They immediately went into action in the invisible world.

We gathered at the president's home on September 5, 1990. I still have a hard time believing what happened there. Instead of a knock-down-drag-out debate, the event more closely resembled a church home-cell group. My battle had been won before we finished our pie. Congeniality and mutual respect was the order of the evening. And since that day, the serious antagonism against teaching and practicing power ministries at Fuller Seminary has disappeared. Not that all the theologians agreed with me, but from then on they did agree that my point of view would be allowed to be taught at Fuller.

What turned the tide? What changed adversity into advantage? It certainly was not my brilliance or my debating skills. Every one of those faculty members had a higher I.Q. than I did. It could only be attributed to intercessors standing in the gap and opening the way for the spiritual environment over the whole institution to be changed.

Are you facing adversity? I recommend that you humble yourself, realize that you cannot go at it alone and activate a powerful prayer shield. Your adversity will become an advantage!

JOURNAL QUESTIONS

1. What kind of adversity have you faced in your personal or professional life? How could you have used humility to help defuse these situations? How could you have turned adversity into advantage?

2. Do any of your lifestyle habits need to change? And would change help you defuse, rather than ignite, adversity?

3. What role does prayer play in defusing adversity?

JOURNAL NOTES

Therefore humble yourselves under the mighty hand of God,
that He may exalt you in due time.

1 PETER 5:6

_____

_____

_____

_____

_____

_____

_____

_____

_____

_____

_____

_____

_____

_____

_____

_____

_____

_____

_____

_____

_____

_____

_____

_____

_____

_____

_____

_____

_____

_____

_____

_____

_____

_____

_____

_____

_____

_____

FOR TO BE CARNALLY MINDED

IS DEATH, BUT TO BE SPIRITUALLY

MINDED IS LIFE AND PEACE.

Romans 8:6

C H A P T E R

8

WE CAN BE
VICTORIOUS!

God would not tell us to do something that was impossible for us to do. That is why I have come to believe that if Jesus told us to humble ourselves, each of us can, in fact, be humble. This does not mean that we can be perfect. It does not mean that we will be the most humble people in the world. It does not mean that we have arrived and that there is nothing we can do to be more humble in the future. But it does mean that we have met God's basic requirements for humility and He, therefore, is ready to keep His promise and exalt us.

WE MAY FACE ROADBLOCKS

I have been comparing the process of humbling ourselves to a trip. If along the road we encounter one of the signposts of pride, we turn and go in a different direction. If we find ourselves passing a signpost of humility, it is a green light that encourages us to move forward.

As we continue ahead on this journey we need to be aware of the two most persistent roadblocks that can stall us and keep us from arriving. They are insecurity and carnality. If you have been striving to move in the direction of humility and if you feel that you are not making the progress that you should, take an honest look at the possible effects of insecurity and carnality in your life.

Insecurity

I have already noted the problems involved with insecurity. In a book on how to humble ourselves as Jesus desires us to do, it would be difficult to overstress insecurity. If we are insecure, we constantly feel that we have something to prove to others. Then when we overcompensate, more times than not we begin to head down the road to pride. We may not always know when we have done this. Sometimes pride is like bad breath—we are usually the last one to know we have it! That is why I do not feel I should end this book without noting these final danger signals—I hope that knowing more about them will keep some people from being blindsided.

There are two major causes of insecurity in a Christian's life. The first is to not fully understand who we are in Christ. It is possible to be born again, to be saved, to be on the way to heaven and yet not to be as aware as we should be of the tremendous advantages we have as believers. God originally created us so that we can enjoy personal fellowship with Him. Before we were Christians, we could not fulfill this destiny. But when we accepted Jesus Christ as Lord and Savior, we were transformed by the power of God into new creatures. We are now members of God's own personal family. We are, therefore, heirs of God's kingdom. This in itself can and should produce an awesome sense of personal security.

Neil Anderson has authored a number of best-selling books, including *Finding Hope Again*, that have helped thousands of Christians gain more freedom than they thought possible, because they had never fully realized who they were in Christ. I recommend these books to anyone who might harbor doubts in this regard.

Another common source of insecurity among Christians is not to know for sure exactly how we fit into the body of Christ. In order to gain confidence as to where we fit in, we need to know what our spiritual gifts are. Every Christian has been given one or more spiritual gifts that equip them to serve as functional members of the body of Christ—just as specifically as our elbows, livers and tongues function as members of our physical bodies.

Believers who have discovered their spiritual gifts and who use them on a regular basis rarely exhibit symptoms of insecurity. They may not be the most vital organs. They may be teeth instead of lungs or ankle bones instead of eyes, but it does not matter. God is the One who has decided which member each one should be and He is the One who has given the necessary gifts to fulfill that particular assignment. As soon as we know what gifts God has given us, insecurity will be less of a problem. We will be fulfilling our God-given destiny.

Believers who have discovered their spiritual gifts and who use them on a regular basis rarely exhibit symptoms of insecurity.

Carnality

The second potential roadblock on the way to humility is carnality. It is possible to be truly saved but also to be carnal. Paul wrote to the Corinthians, "I, brethren, could not speak to you as to spiritual people, but as to carnal, as to babes in Christ" (1 Cor. 3:1). Carnal people end up exhibiting more of the works of the flesh than the fruit of the Spirit. And the work of the flesh that most directly derails humility is pride.

If we are proud, we have a tendency to prove ourselves superior to others by criticizing them and jockeying them into a position of inferiority. We can actually convince ourselves that we are serving God by tearing others down. One of my pet peeves is magazines and journals which expect those who review the books of others to spend the last paragraph or two finding fault with the book. Instead of being positive, reviews must always end on a negative note. This really amounts to the reviewer saying, in effect, "If the author of this book were only as smart as I am, it would be a better book."

WHY CRITICIZE OTHERS?

In an attempt to avoid carnality, I have a longstanding policy of not criticizing by name those with whom I may disagree. I do not mind examining the positives and negatives of ideas, and, at times, I have quite vigorously done so. However, personal polemics is not now my style, even though it was when I was younger. Some of my academic colleagues seem to become irritated with me on this point, because a critical mind is regarded as a badge of distinction among them. I remember that awhile ago, several academics took me on by name, disagreeing with my views on strategic-level spiritual warfare. I was then invited to respond to these critics at an annual meeting of the Evangelical Missiological Society. I am afraid that I disappointed most of those who attended the session when I dealt only with ideas, refusing to put on the gloves and attack by name those individuals who had criticized me. The reason that I do not do this is that I feel it is a carnal approach and that it takes me in a direction opposite of humility.

The remedy for carnality is holiness. I believe that it is possible for us to live lives that are not characterized by sin. The Bible informs us, "But as he who called you is holy, you also be holy in all your conduct" (1 Pet. 1:15). God expects us to be holy. He can enable us to go a full day or more without sinning. Not that we are ever exempt from the possibility of sinning, but when we do sin we confess it, He forgives us and we move ahead with a clean slate.

Humility and Holiness

So few Christians these days outwardly profess to live a consistently holy life that those who say they do might be accused of being proud of their holiness. But holiness and humility are not conflicting ideals; they go together. Being humble is part and parcel of being holy—and God expects both.

Think of Paul as an example. He asserted that he was humble: "I, Paul, myself am pleading with you by the meekness [humility] and gentleness of Christ" (2 Cor. 10:1). He also affirmed his holiness: "You are witnesses, and God also, how devoutly and justly and blamelessly we behaved ourselves among you who believe" (1 Thess. 2:10).

WE CAN BE VICTORIOUS!

Watch out for the potential roadblocks of insecurity and carnality. If we know about them, we can move forward on the road to humility. Since it is the will of God that we arrive at our destination on this road, we can certainly end up victorious! We can be exalted!

Whoever exalts himself

- **will be humbled,**

and whoever humbles himself

- **will be exalted!**

JOURNAL QUESTIONS

1. In what ways are insecurity and carnality roadblocks to becoming humble? What are the roadblocks in your life?

2. How is humility related to holiness? Are there ways you can be more meek and express the gentleness of Christ?

JOURNAL NOTES

The humble will rejoice in the LORD.
ISAIAH 29:19, *NIV*

_____

_____

_____

_____

_____

_____

_____

_____

NOTES

Chapter 1

1. *The Open Bible, New King James Version,* expanded edition (Nashville, TN: Thomas Nelson Publishers, 1983), p. 303.
2. Ibid.

Chapter 2

1. Andrew Murray, *Humility* (New Kensington, PA: Whitaker House, 1982), p. 51.
2. George Barna, *The Second Coming of the Church* (Nashville, TN: Word Publishing, 1998), pp. 120-121.
3. Murray, *Humility,* p. 43.
4. Ibid., p. 68.
5. Ibid., pp. 27-30.

Chapter 3

1. A. A. MacRae, *Numbers: The New Bible Commentary,* ed. F. Davidson (London, England: Inter-Varsity Fellowship, 1953), p. 177.
2. John Bevere, "Humility," *Messenger,* vol. 1 (2001), p. 2.
3. *Webster's New Universal Unabridged Dictionary,* s. v. "humble."

Chapter 4

1. Robert J. Furey, *So I'm Not Perfect: A Psychology of Humility* (New York: Alba House, 1986), p. xii.
2. John W. Yates III, "Pottering and Prayer," *Christianity Today* (April 2, 2001), p. 60.
3. Ibid.

4. Eddie Hyatt, "Pitfalls of Revival: Maintaining Humility During Times of Blessing," *Arise* (summer 2000), p. 43.

5. Ibid.

Chapter 5

1. *Webster's New Universal Unabridged Dictionary*, s. v. "pride."
2. Andrew Murray, *Humility* (New Kensington, PA: Whitaker House, 1982), p. 20.
3. Robert J. Furey, *So I'm Not Perfect: A Psychology of Humility* (New York: Alba House, 1986), p. 18.
4. Ralph and Gretchen Mahoney, "Apostles/Prophets Working Together," *World MAP Digest*, p. 6.
5. Richard J. Foster, "Growing Together," *Renovaré*, vol. 11, no. 2 (April 2001), n.p.
6. Murray, *Humility*, pp. 46-47.
7. Ibid., p. 50.

Chapter 6

1. John W. Yates III, "Pottering and Prayer," *Christianity Today* (April 2, 2001) pp. 60-61.
2. Donald McGavran's description of the homogeneous unit principle: "People like to become Christians without crossing racial, linguistic or class barriers." Donald A. McGavran, *Understanding Church Growth*, ed. C. Peter Wagner, third edition revised (Grand Rapids, MI: William B. Eerdmans Publishing, 1990), p. 163.
3. For the record, an extensive summary and analysis of the homogeneous unit principle debate has been written by my Fuller Seminary colleague Charles Van Engen in *Planting Multiethnic Congregations in North America* (Chicago: Trinity Evangelical Divinity School, Ted Ward Consultation on the Development and Nurture of Multiethnic Congregations, 1997).
4. David Lowell Cook, "The Americanization of the Church Growth Movement," *Journal of the American Society for Church Growth*, vol. 11 (fall 2000), pp. 15-50.
5. Andrew Murray, *Humility* (New Kensington, PA: Whitaker House, 1982), p. 65.
6. Ibid.

Chapter 7

1. Ted Haggard, *Primary Purpose* (Lake Mary, FL: Creation House, 1995), p. 58.

Make Your Daily Life Your Great Adventure

God's Secret to Greatness
The Power of the Towel
David Cape and *Tommy Tenney*
Paperback
ISBN 08307.25873

Somebody Cares
A Guide to Living
Out Your Faith
Doug Stringer
Paperback
ISBN 08307.28600
Video
UPC 607135.005889

Who I Am in Christ
A Devotional
Neil T. Anderson
Paperback
ISBN 08307.28902

Our Daily Walk
Starting Your Day with Jesus
Jack Hayford
Paperback
ISBN 18524.01923

Living the Spirit-Formed Life
Growing in the 10 Principles
of Spirit-Filled Discipleship
Jack Hayford
Paperback
ISBN 08307.27671
Video
UPC 607135.005452

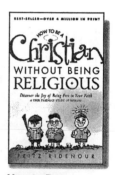

How to Be a Christian Without Being Religious
Discover the Joy of
Being Free in Your Faith
Fritz Ridenour
Paperback
ISBN 08307.27892

Regal
GOD'S WORD FOR YOUR WORLD

Available at your local Christian bookstore
www.regalbooks.com

043180

Also from
C. Peter Wagner

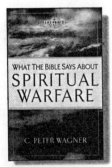
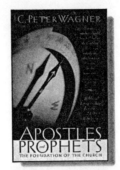

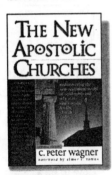